DEEP

FOUNDATIONAL

DELIVERANCE

SECRET TO SPIRITUAL WARFARE

Life is Spiritual; the one who is careful about the spiritual realm is the one who will overcome it.

DR. PHILOMENA

GERALD ISHENGOMA

ISBN

Hardcover: 978-1-969120-09-1

Paperback: 978-1-969120-08-4

"If the foundations are destroyed, what can the righteous do?"

(Psalms 11:3)

Table of Contents

Introduction

A life that cries for deliverance but never receives it is a life shackled in an invisible prison, a soul drowning in affliction with no lifeline in sight. It is a journey marked by unrelenting pain, a ceaseless war fought on unseen battlefields where the enemy is relentless and the victim is unaware of the chains that bind them. The walls close tighter each day, yet there is no door, escape, or light breaking through the darkness. Such a life is one where confusion reigns supreme.

A person wakes each morning only to find the same torment awaiting them, a mundane cycle that refuses to be broken. Nothing ever truly works; relationships crumble, opportunities slip through their fingers, health deteriorates, and peace remains a distant dream. Every effort to rise is met with an unseen force pulling them down; every step forward is met with an inexplicable setback. And so, they wander in circles, their destiny hijacked, their purpose distorted, their strength drained by unseen forces that have claimed dominion over their existence.

It is a tragic reality where joy is a fleeting illusion, a momentary glimpse of what could be before it is mercilessly snatched away. A person in need of deliverance laughs but is not truly happy, smiles but carries unbearable weight within. Sleep brings no rest, for even the night is filled with torment whispers in the dark, shadows that loom, and nightmares that do not fade with the morning light. The air around them feels heavy, like the weight of a thousand unseen chains drags them deeper into despair. A mind afflicted by this bondage is never free. It is haunted by thoughts that are not its own, plagued by fears that refuse to

1

be silenced. Anxiety grips like a vice, depression becomes a second skin, and hopelessness carves its way into the soul. They look around, searching for answers, but find none. The world moves on, oblivious to their suffering, while they remain trapped in a reality where the unseen dictates their fate.

Sickness becomes a companion, a relentless affliction that no medicine can cure. Doctors diagnose, treatments are given, but healing never comes. The body weakens, drained not just by physical ailments but by spiritual battles waged beyond the reach of human understanding. Finances crumble inexplicably, no matter how hard they labor, as if a devourer has set its sights on all they possess. Doors that should open remain shut, the flow of favor is blocked, and blessings that should come are intercepted before they ever reach their intended recipients. And then there is loneliness.

Oh, the loneliness. It is an isolation that cannot be explained, an exile in a crowd. Relationships can turn sour without apparent cause, loved ones can become distant, and friendships can wither like flowers starved of water. No one understands; no one sees the battles fought silently, the unheard cries. Even the most potent love seems unable to break the invisible barrier that separates them from the rest of the world.

As you continue reading, I ask that you remain open to all the revelations the Lord is about to reveal. Do not trivialize them; believe them in faith, and you will begin to see tremendous victories and results in your life by the power of God.

Chapter 1:
If Foundations Are Destroyed, What Can the Righteous Do?

Deep Foundational Deliverance

Looking at the book of Jeremiah 1:10.

In this book about deliverance, we will focus on the Bible, and our anchor scripture will be Jeremiah 1:10, as it lays the foundation for deep, foundational deliverance. Many Christians understand Jeremiah 1:10 in part, and that is why accessing total deliverance has been a challenge. For a few that are delivered, the deliverance is most likely incomplete. When you see people delivered at a crusade, it is partial; the goal of that deliverance is to sustain that person in their pursuit of total and complete deliverance. Pursuing total deliverance is crucial for every believer, as the Bible states that deliverance is the children's bread. So, deliverance is waiting for us; we must know of it and begin pursuing it in Jesus' name. One who is totally and wholly delivered can be used as a vessel to deliver everyone else God has sent their way. Every servant of God must deliver themselves before they begin a deliverance ministry. You cannot have a deliverance ministry if you are not delivered.

Personally, I never thought I would have to discuss foundational deliverance one day. As a medical doctor, this was far below my list of things I could pursue here on Earth. The number one reason why? My daily schedule was already full, and I had no room to add one more thing, such as addressing deep or foundational deliverance.

I was born and raised in a deeply rooted well-respected Catholic family that passionately loved the Lord. My family had a daily schedule for God, apart from everything else. A typical day would begin at 6 am in the church before work and conclude at 8 pm with a night prayer. My parents did everything humanly possible to raise us in the fear of God, and I can attest that my family is one of those Sons of God, totally sold out for Jesus. I am referring to the entire family— my grandparents, parents, siblings, and the current generation pertaining to my family tree.

However, as we grew older, I came to realize many things I had not understood or taken note of since I was younger. For example, addiction of all kinds, alcohol, drugs, then hard life, poverty, transgenerational curses, disobedience, liberion to the orders of God even though still going to church, broken marriages, broken families, broken children. People were dying prematurely. Every year, we would bury one or two people, usually young people. It hurt so bad, but then I heard my people say it was the will of God. So, I don't know how to end this painful '*Will of God*'.

We continued burying young people, and then it came to my own family. My dad died at 44, my mom died at 46, my young sister died at 8, and my brother, the oldest child, died at 36. Even though I am a medical doctor, I could put all the diagnoses down and try to make sense of them to have peace and closure. But my heart did not settle, I needed to have a discussion with God on this matter, I needed to know what can I do to stop this once and for all?

At the age of 18, immediately after high school, as the second-born only girl among seven children in the family, I officially took on the role of a parent. Raising my brothers. By the Grace of God, I was selected to attend a medical school, which I was sponsored by a God-sent angel.

The small amount of money I was given to pay for my school fees and living expenses, I also used to take my own brothers to school abroad from secondary school in Uganda to University in India, while still schooling myself abroad. However, I was originally born and raised in Tanzania. This is where the saying of; "you raise a girl, you raise a village" comes in— *that is me.*

I had questions, but there was no one there to answer them. Parents are gone, family friends are away, and relatives are busy with their own families. This was the most painful journey for a 19-year-old girl! I said, '*God, there's more to this.*' Little did I know that God was preparing me for Revival, starting from my own foundation, but the cleanup has to start somewhere, right?

I prayed to God to show me a clearer path for everywhere was filled with darkness. Something did not make sense in my foundation. Even the people whom I spent money to educate, the devil did not leave them alone; he still pursued them. He would not allow them to stabilize in their career and families. Instead, "They fell into drugs, fornication, alcohol, and disobeyed the Lord. A wasting spirit and a vagabond spirit were released upon them. The foundational battle could no longer be hidden. A curse, poverty continued to follow them. Their lives were indeed challenged. "But God, in His mercy, will always look to preserve His seed. He will choose one person to deliver the oppressed. I believe that person is me." If by any chance you happen to be reading this book, then, that is you. You are called to deliver the oppressed. Just as it is written in Isaiah 6:8 'Then I heard the voice of the Lord saying, "Whom shall I send? And who will go for us?" And I said, "Here am I Lord. Send me!"' I respond with a willing heart. In my case, as a medical doctor and a mother of 4 children now, my first pregnancy, I conceived twin boys, but only one survived. Despite my loss, I still thanked God for what I gained. After that, I had a couple of mysterious miscarriages

5

consecutively. I thanked God thinking it is the will of God. Then I conceived again at exactly 4 months, my cervix was not competent to hold the baby as the baby grew. It was continually opening. I was on total bed rest, which means the baby could not survive; there was no hope. I ran to God, I cried, I prayed. God heard me and kept my baby beyond doctors' knowledge and understanding, allowing me to bring her into this world.

The next pregnancy, my son was born a healthy baby, but the enemy tried to snatch away my baby exactly at 4 months old. I had to run back to God in anguish and speak a language that only I and God could understand. God heard me, and that is how my child recovered from terrible sudden mysterious severe satanic attack that took down his life, where Doctors have given up, but God in His mercy brought him back to life. I remember that moment as it was yesterday, inside of me I was speaking 'I will not bury my seed over satanic command' I will not mourn over satanic command, I refuse, it will not be in the record that Satan had victory over my child also as he did to other family members. I stood bold, I said no Satan, this far, no further, enough is enough, my child was brought back to life, death has been swallowed in victory.

This is when I realised that God is with me, where man has put a full stop that is where God began a new sentence. Since that time, the way I see the Lord has completely changed. I made up my mind to seek this God with all my heart and all my soul. Jeremiah 29:13 *"You will seek Me and find Me when you search for Me with all your heart."* Now as this situation changed me, at this moment my heart wants to know Him the Yahweh and the power of His resurrection. Philippians 3:10 It was at that moment I knew without a doubt that God is real and He is with me more than ever before.

Again, in my 4th pregnancy, exactly at 4 months of pregnancy, during a normal prenatal check-up, the doctor couldn't find a heartbeat. They referred me to a more qualified radiologist. Still no heartbeat. I left the appointment crying, unsure of what to do next. I went home. I wanted to reach out to my Lord, but I didn't know what to even ask for. I realised that my battle was bigger than what I know or seen before and this must be more of spiritual, but I didn't know how to go about it. A dark hopelessness took over me again. I just surrendered myself to Jesus and said let your will be done Lord."

I asked and begged God, saying, "*God, what really is it? For sure,* because when I thought that the battle was over, it was just the beginning of another new battle, *there is more to this story. What is it? Speak to me, God, and reveal to me what this is.* Two days later, I felt a little movement in my belly. I rushed to the hospital, and after a check-up, the doctors told me my child was alive. It was at this point that I realized something I did not understand was controlling my life, something bigger than me.

My mindset shifted. There was an awakening. I didn't know what was causing this negativity and repeated cycles, but I wanted to find out. I began to pursue the Lord more than ever. I started fasting and praying at midnight, which is how I landed in the *Deliverance Ministry* — the rest is history.

It was almost as if my covenant with God had been renewed. The Bible says, *'You shall know the truth, and the truth shall set you free.'* I was angry in my spirit and I needed all the truth I could gather.

In my stillness, clearly, I heard the Lord said Exodus 14:14 The Lord will fight for you, you need only to be still. I began to reflect on all the complications I had during ALL my pregnancies. As I asked the Lord why, I heard Him say, 'This is nothing but the battle of the womb, the battle of the chosen. Your children are chosen they carry the scepter for territories and nations. That is why the enemy is so vicious toward your seed. But My hand is upon you and your children. They are Mine. The enemy may try, but he will not succeed.' The Lord then led me to read Revelation 12:4–6."

Revelation 12:4–6:

"The dragon stood before the woman who was about to give birth, so that when she gave birth, he might devour her child. She gave birth to a son, a male child, who is to rule all the nations with a rod of iron and the woman fled into the wilderness where she had a place prepared by God.

In my mind, I heard the Lord say that there are things He cannot show me until I am ready. I didn't know how ready God wanted me to be, beyond attending church, worshiping, praying, giving, and loving people. I didn't know what else to do to be ready.

God said, *'You could be doing so many things for God, while God is not involved in what you do.'* A good example is Martha and her sister Mary in the Bible, when Jesus visited them in the village of Bethany. Martha was busy in the house, perhaps cooking or preparing something for Jesus, but we see Mary sitting at Jesus' feet, accessing intimacy with Christ, which Martha thought was a sign of laziness. But the truth is, Mary was drinking from the fountain. That is why when Martha complained to Jesus, Jesus answered Martha, *"Your sister Mary has done the right thing."* As painful as the journey was, God still needed me to sit at His feet for him to be able to reveal deep foundational secrets and deliver the broken foundation.

During the course of your life, for God to give you deep secrets of life, you need to sit at His feet and access intimacy with Him. In my case, I needed an answer. What I realized is that to obtain that answer, I had to seek the Lord with all my heart. Now, I ask God to lead me.

I speak to God that, even now, I may not understand everything, but I assure you, Lord, that I am ready for you to reveal what is happening in my life. I give you permission Lord take charge over me, disclose hidden agendas of the enemy and lead my foundation to deliverance and freedom.

The Lord took me to a quote— *scripture* Jeremiah 33:3 ***"Call to me, and I will answer you and tell you great and unsearchable things you do not know."*** I said, *Lord, I am ready; I am knocking, and I am calling.* Now, God began to read my heart and understood that I was interested in learning and knowing more of the mysteries in my foundation.

The core mystery remained untouched even my education offered no answers, and even the mighty vessels of God stood silent before my questions. Consistent prayers and fasting could not answer my questions. I had no options but to return to the one who created me and my family; I knew he would answer me. As I began to take my relationship with the Lord seriously, paying attention to every detail that God taught me through the Holy Spirit and the Word of God, I realized that God was indeed speaking to me. I was filled with the Holy Spirit; I could hear the Voice of God clear no matter how whispering it was, I would listen. This brought me so much joy because it was at this point that I realized God was real. No man could have brought me to this point except God Himself. My dreamland opened, before this I could dream and not remember, or remember partially, and God began to reveal things to me in the dream;

9

the voice of God became the most significant asset in my daily life. I began to develop a deeper interest in things of God.

"So, God began to answer my questions about my foundation, revealing to me that this is a battle of the foundation. What I had been seeing as manifestations were only the surface shallow signs of a much deeper issue. There are evil foundations and hidden plantations that have existed for generations, passed down from one to another. No one ever stopped to ask how to uproot them."

I heard God tell me, Psalms 11:3 "*If the foundations are being destroyed, what can the righteous do?*" And He gave me the answer right away: "*The righteous will rebuild the destroyed foundation.*" If the walls are broken, what can the righteous do? The righteous will rebuild the broken walls. And that is exactly what Nehemiah did. Return to the roots, investigate, put a diagnosis and rebuild. That is what God told me. I didn't know how to do this apart from the one I already knew and had done, which didn't work. I still had questions because I didn't know how I would start this journey of rebuilding the broken walls. Then I heard the Lord clearly saying, "*I am the one to build the broken walls, but I need you to commit yourself to me totally*".

He gave me James 4:7: **Submit yourselves totally to the Lord; resist the devil, and he will flee from you.** God told me that without James 4:7, dealing with the foundation and rebuilding the broken walls is impossible. I said, '*Lord, I am ready; help me help this soul, spirit, and body learn how to submit.* ' *Teach me how to humble myself; teach me how to submit honestly. As for me, I give you my everything. I submit wholeheartedly. Please, God, accept this as my sacrifice to you. As for me and my household, we shall serve the Lord.*

Then the Lord said to me, *"See, I have set you this day over nations and kingdoms to pluck up and to break down, to destroy and to overthrow, to build and to plant."* Jeremiah 1:10 God made it clear to me that I must put this scripture into practice for foundational, deep deliverance. "God made it clear that there can be no true foundational deliverance without Jeremiah 1:10 and without a committed platform of consistency and discipline in continuous prayer." Only through persistent prayer can the deep roots of a faulty foundation be truly uprooted." That was the key I needed to start the journey of deep foundational deliverance. That was how I started.

I recall that at the time, the Lord began to open my eyes, and the Spirit of God led me to the *University of Heaven*, right here on earth, to teach me things that no man could have taught me. I had looked everywhere but could not find any help, and no one told me that if the foundation is destroyed, a righteous man would need to sit down, submit to God, and start building the broken foundation as God directs. This requires spending more time with God, but many of us would rather spend time with *men of God* than with *God*, and this was also my case. But I thank God that He delivered me from relying on men and helped me focus more on the Cross and Jesus.

"Moreover, God revealed to me that many of the so-called men of God whom people rely on are not truly delivered. They live in sin and have normalized it from their pulpits engaging in fornication, lying, manipulation, and even stealing from members through the prosperity gospel. Some go as far as impregnating members and ordering abortions for rituals and sacrifices, yet they still prophesy and appear genuine. Many have turned their congregations into worshipers of themselves, treating them as if they were

11

small gods. But only God only Jesus is to be worshiped, not any man."

But the Lord made it clear: the way to discern them is by the presence of sin in their lives. The signs and wonders they display come from the kingdom of darkness. The Lord said, 'The signs and wonders that come from Me are always accompanied by holiness, righteousness, the fear of the Lord, and purity. There is no room for compromise.'

"If someone claims to be delivered but still lives in sin, that person has not truly been delivered. One crucial sign of genuine deliverance is a deep fear of sin. True deliverance requires effort it is a spiritual labor. You cannot work hard to be delivered only to return to the very sin you were freed from. Deliverance means you have sacrificed and paid a price that no one can place a value on. A truly delivered person lives a disciplined life, marked by holiness, righteousness, purity and self-control."

God told me, 'I have departed from many churches. What you see men or women of God doing is often just their personal experience not My anointing.' At that moment, my eyes were opened. I became desperate for God to reveal even more to me."

The beautiful thing about spending more time with God is that when you make yourself available to Him, He eagerly draws near. He nourishes you with the food of the Spirit which is the word of God, and you will never thirst again. He opens divine scrolls, unveils hidden mysteries, and clothes you in His glory and power, anointing you for His purpose.

Every time you are in a secret place with God, you can never be the same; you emerge from the secret place as a new person. If there is anything I desire, it is to stay more in the secret place with Christ. If many understood this, they would pursue the Lord more than men because God will give you what no man can. I pray that in this faith journey; you will seek the Lord and spend more time in the secret place with the Lord than anything else. May you be delivered, in Jesus' name, from everything that distracts and keeps you from dwelling in the secret place with Christ Jesus. Amen.

As I stayed closer and closer to God, I remembered my need was deep, foundational deliverance; however, I had already diagnosed my case with God, and He had told me that my issue had to do with a faulty foundation. God clarified that it has nothing to do with my parents or grandparents, whom I have witnessed serving the Lord with fear and love. But somewhere in the foundation, an evil root remained hidden, silent, that had not been properly uprooted, and that was my assignment: to discover the source of the disorder and, without fail, eradicate it once and for all.

Deep, foundational deliverance: The Lord gave me directions to pay attention to the details of Jeremiah 1:10, indicating that every portion of the six things mentioned must be taken care of if I want total and complete deep foundational deliverance. Jeremiah 1:10 says, ***See. I have given you power to uproot, tear down, destroy, overthrow, build, and plant, saith the lord.*** Most believers have skipped the portion of Jeremiah 1:10 (uproot, tear down, destroy, and overthrow) because it is the most challenging part, but they can do the last two portions of Jeremiah 1:10 (build and plant). Building and planting are the easiest parts.

But the question is, if you choose to build and plant, on which foundation is you planting? Which foundation are you building on? I believe as children of God, no matter how much we try and avoid these first four parts (uproot, tear down, destroy, and overthrow), which are the most

13

important for everyone who is pursuing deep foundational deliverance, things of the foundational will still be against us or hurt us because we are building on a faulty foundation. Therefore, the most important thing to do before building and planting is to examine Psalms 11:3, which states, *If their foundations are destroyed, what can a righteous person do?* So, who is the righteous man? The righteous person is you a child of God who has been born again and is a believer, loving God and their foundation.

As believers, we have overlooked the foundational issue, even though we believe it has been destroyed. How do we know the foundations are destroyed? By examining our family background, we can explore the roots of our heritage, including our forefathers and ancestors. However, if we say we have received Jesus and we begin to build and plant on a faulty foundation without cleaning our faulty foundation, the Bible says,

> *Matthew 7:24-26: "Therefore, everyone who hears these words of mine and puts them into practice is like a wise man who built his house on the rock." The rain came down, the streams rose, and the winds blew and beat against that house; yet it did not fall, because it had its foundation on the rock. But everyone who hears these words of mine and does not put them into practice is like a foolish man who built his house on sand."*

In many cases, believers have taken refuge under the covering of Jesus's blood, yet remain unwilling to confront the foundational issues that have been left unaddressed for generations. These unresolved roots are what continue to wound families, community, the church and the nation as a whole. Remember if the people are not willing to be delivered at the family level, then the community is ruined, the church is ruined, the nation is also ruined.

The blood of Jesus, the power of resurrection, and the power of the cross are your pass-through salvation, as a child of God to utilize it, from the beginning of the journey of deliverance all the way to the courts of heaven, where you need to demand what is rightfully yours and needs to be released to you. But many of us don't do that; it is because we have been taught that since Jesus died for us, it is all finished. Yes, I agree, but that does not discount the things of the forefathers, which the Bible says.

> *Jeremiah 31:28 Just as I watched over them to uproot and tear down, and to overthrow, destroy and bring disaster, so I will watch over them to build and to plant," declares the LORD.*
>
> *Jeremiah 31:29: "In those days people will no longer say, 'The parents have eaten sour grapes, and the children's teeth are set on edge.'*

God is expecting us to revisit our foundation and do the right thing: remove dark kingdoms that our forefathers served out of ignorance and bring in the Kingdom of light, our Lord Jesus Christ. As our forefathers served the kingdom of darkness, they put some legal satanic covenants in place that are still active and speaking. Unless one comes to understand this and begins to address the foundation, these powers when Christ is forcefully introduced without confronting them will resist and oppress the people of God. Why? Because they retain legal rights to operate within the framework of that untouched foundation.

The legal covenant in place is to serve Satan, and you want to serve Jesus without following the legal steps of leaving their kingdom because, according to the covenant, you are still part of them; you are their bloodline, you are their child. Whatever they are doing will still affect you unless you take legal steps to sever your ties with them. This is accomplished by confessing, repenting, renouncing, and asking for cleansing from the Lord Jesus Christ. Sadly, many believers have not taken these steps, largely because this truth is rarely taught or spoken about in many churches today across the globe. That is why so many are hurt by the foundational issues and don't know what to do about them. God is here to help us navigate through and overcome the powers of the foundational battles.

The Bible says in 1 John 3:8: ***For this purpose, the Son of God was manifested, that He might destroy the works of the devil.***

This verse is in New Testament after Jesus, which means that even after Jesus came, there were still some works of the devil that had to be destroyed. Still, there has to be a vessel to be used to destroy these works of Satan. That vessel is you and me through the blood of Jesus, through the power of resurrection, through the power of the cross, through the word of God, and applying legal rights through the word of God to demand our rights as believers through the proper steps of confession, renunciation, and repentance and asking for cleansing by the mercies of God.

This is what you need to do to destroy the works of Satan, not through anointed oil, anointed water, anointed handkerchiefs, or prophecies that make you excited, jump up and down. These are satanic manipulations meant to distract believers from focusing on the true course that brings complete deliverance.

Today, the church has evolved into a venue for entertainment, business, and motivational speaking. All of this is a lie from the enemy. It is not helping anyone. Day by day, both the church and the believer are drifting further away from God's true agenda for the pulpit.

Why do we need to follow the appropriate process? It is because we do not want to overstep jurisdiction; we do not want to bypass protocols and overstep boundaries through self-righteousness, as the scriptures say,

> **Matthew 5:25 NKJV:** *Agree with your adversary quickly, while you are on the way with him, lest your adversary deliver you to the judge, the judge hands you over to the officer, and you be imprisoned.*

Christians have ignored this kind of knowledge; that is why we have seen many lives being destroyed and going down day after day, even though they are children of God. One's life being destroyed by negative cycles, patterns, destroyed destinies, premature death, being harassed and tormented by demons and spirits, sickness, infirmities, diseases, destroyed Christian families, poverty, divorce, hopelessness, etc.

It doesn't matter how much you pray, fast, and consecrate yourself; the problem keeps getting deeper and deeper. All this is because a legal right is in place, an open door exists, and no one wants to deal with it. Many children of God are left with unanswered questions; "Many church leaders whom we look up to for answers and relief from our pain are themselves hurting. Some are going through divorce, family chaos, addiction, gender confusion, afflictions, premature death, and repeated cycles of struggle. They often have to gather the strength just to stand on the pulpit and encourage others while there is no one to encourage them." many don't know who to ask or where to run to. Some even think God has abandoned them, while some believe God's word is a lie to the point of accusing God and losing hope. Some have chosen to accept their negative situation, claiming it is the will of God. I grew up seeing my people hurt by losing young family members, and saying it is the will of God.

It was I who came to overturn the narrative, saying that every negative thing that is happening is NOT the will of God. There are some undiscovered mysteries in the foundation that have been left untouched. God started unveiling the hidden mysteries of iniquity in my family and foundation. That's how we began to address issues like premature death. It stopped completely. The family tree that used to bury 2 to 3 people a year since the 1980s due to inequity stopped in 2014, and from 2014 to 2025, there have been no premature deaths. Praise be to God. I sang Hallelujah, Amen, Salvation, power, and glory belong to our God! Amen. I wish I had known this knowledge before; my family would have not lost many lives prematurely by the devil.

Thanks be to God Almighty, who taught me deep things. God brought the University of Heaven right here on earth through the Holy Spirit and began to teach me what I need to know and to act. The Bible says:

> *John 14:26: "But the Helper, the Holy Spirit, whom the Father will send in my name, will teach you all things and bring to your remembrance all that I have said to you." He is our teacher, the Holy Spirit."*

The Holy Spirit is considered the primary teacher of God's people, teaching us about God, ourselves, and how to live as holy Christians, benefiting every aspect of God's advantage right here on earth without being interfered with by Satan. My life is a living testimony; as the Holy Spirit teaches me, I can attest that it works. The Holy Spirit has guided me slowly and carefully through this journey and is the one who has been teaching and directing me. Remember, the Holy Spirit only teaches those who are willing to learn. If you believe you've figured it all out if you think you know the Bible from Genesis to Revelation and consider yourself too spiritually elevated to be taught then you've already disqualified yourself from His instruction. And if the Holy Spirit can't teach you, forget about being filled by Him. The Holy Spirit imparts only to the humble and hates the proud. James 4:6. But the grace that God gives is even stronger. *"God resists the proud but gives grace to the humble.* "In the time we live in today, everyone who desires to do the work of God must seek to be filled with the Holy Spirit. The Bible says that those who are born of the Spirit are like the wind this means the Spirit leads them beyond human understanding. The Holy Spirit is always on standby, ready to move through a vessel of God who responds to His command." **John 3:8** *"The wind blows where it wishes, and you hear the sound of it, but cannot tell where it comes from and where it goes. So is everyone who is born of the Spirit."*

"I've had many people tell me that they've been in church for a long time, yet they are still not filled with the Holy Spirit." One way to attract the Holy Spirit to dwell in you is by cultivating the right heart posture and life attitude. What draws the Holy Spirit is not outward appearance, but the condition of the heart. A pure and humble heart, broken in repentance, draws Him near, as seen in *Psalm 51:17.* Holiness and a desire to live righteously are also essential, for *Hebrews 12:14* reminds us that without holiness, no one will see the Lord. Obedience to God's Word creates a welcoming environment for the Spirit, as Jesus said in *John 14:23*: "If anyone loves me, he will obey my teaching and my Father will love them and we will come to him and make our home with him."

A deep hunger and thirst for God, like that described in *Matthew 5:6*, invites His presence. Additionally, a lifestyle of prayer and worship, as seen in *Acts 13:2*, opens the door for the Holy Spirit to speak and move. Finally, faith and expectation are crucial; *Hebrews 11:6* declares that without faith, it is impossible to please God. The Holy Spirit is drawn to those who not only seek Him but also believe that He will come.

Chapter 2:
The Holy Spirit

I truly believe this is a time for every thoughtful believer to seek the Spirit of the living God, because the season we're in goes beyond what human understanding can grasp. You need the Spirit of God to stay with you and lead you. The Spirit of the Lord can easily rest on a person through generating intimacy with the Lord.

How do you generate intimacy with the Lord? *Be discipled* in the Lord and Maintain discipline in the things of the Lord, such as reading the Word of the Lord, and consistency in your actions related to your *God given destiny and* the assignment God has given you here on earth. You can deepen your intimacy with God by stirring up His fire through prayer and simply spending a bit more time in His presence. *Additionally, "Purity is also essential for anyone who desires to be a vessel of the Holy Spirit and to cultivate deeper intimacy with the Lord. If you truly seek the presence of the Holy Spirit, let holiness and righteousness become part of your daily life. In doing so, you become a temple of God worthy to host His glory and the Holy Spirit will naturally rest upon you."*

This is the path of those ready to humble themselves and have a childlike spirit. You must come with a childlike heart, as Psalm 51:17 suggests, a heart of obedience. 1 Samuel 15:22, Obedience is better than sacrifice, so obedience is the greatest sacrifice to every believer. Jesus suffered so that we may have life in abundance. After God spoke to me through His Word, I started to reflect and ask myself: Is there something missing in my family line? What could it be? As children of God, we shouldn't still be living in suffering because the Bible tells us that when Jesus suffered and died, He took everything to the cross; the curse was taken on the cross, the Bible says. Isaiah 53:4 states, *"Surely he took up our pain and bore our suffering.*

That means that, as believers, we need to live a life filled with God's promises. To live a satisfying life as children of God. However, many believers' lives are the opposite; they are marked by infirmity, sickness, disease, rejection, hatred, poverty, financial crisis, barrenness, or the ancestral powers of the father's house overpowering them. All kinds of spirits are flooding into the lives of many believers. The more you pray, the more these spirits find their way in; they come in as a flood. This means that even your obedience to the Lord, as demonstrated by prayer and fasting, irritates them. However, the answer is simple here. The answer is:

Psalm 11:3 If foundations are destroyed, what can the righteous do?

You are the righteous of the Lord; you have received Jesus; you are filled with the Holy Spirit. You have already entered into a covenant with the Lord Jesus Christ, so you are the one the Lord is waiting for to start working on Jeremiah 1:10, tearing down the deep roots that have been ignored from one generation to the next. Destroying the roots depends on how deep they have grown. The root could be deep if no one in the family has ever taken the family tree seriously for deliverance. There must always be a person, a vessel God uses as a point of contact to deliver that family tree. I pray that if no one in your foundation ever does that, may the Lord give you the grace to take on this project very seriously so that people in your family tree can be delivered and worship the Lord in truth and in Spirit.

But before the rain comes there has to be a man to till the ground. Genesis 2:5 And every plant of the field before it was in the earth, and every herb of the field before it grew: for the LORD God had not caused it to rain upon the earth, and *there was* not a man to till the ground. Many of God given promises has been delayed in many foundations or families or nations because there is no serious man to till the ground. I pray that, you will be the one in Jesus' name, Amen.

First Generational Commander

Being a first-generation commander means you're the first in your bloodline to confront and break foundational strongholds no one before you has done that kind of deliverance work.

This means the roots of inequity are more profound, and each root has branches. Just imagine for a moment that each root has branches according to the generations one carries. That's how deep the roots are. This means that in the first generation, the roots were not uprooted; in the second generation, the roots were not uprooted and instead grew even deeper, with more roots, resulting in a doubling of the root numbers; in the third generation, the roots have tripled in depth and number. As a first-generation commander, you will encounter significant work and numerous challenges if you are unfamiliar with this knowledge, you may be swimming in unending back-to-back battles that overwhelms you.

The powers of your father's house will be challenging you because they never expected that God could use one of their own to challenge them. So, they will try to fight you, but the Lord is with you as you take on the journey. Someone must arise and do this; we can't all keep running and abandoning our inheritance while our people suffer from one hardship to another. Although many people go through deliverance, it's often only partial, and the freedom doesn't always last. To achieve complete and total deliverance, one must return to one's foundation the roots. I am one of them and am a living testimony. There were things that I thought would never break at all. But I kept holding onto the word of God that says,

> ### *James 4:7 Submit to the Lord. Resist the devil, and he shall flee from you.*

I didn't like the situation where the enemy hurt me, tormented me, and mocked me, my family, and my children. That's when I decided to delve deeper and began researching and investigating my family background, and then I discovered that I came from a flawed foundation. No one had gone ahead of me to deal with my faulty foundation. All my family members were regular churchgoers, religious, devout Christians, or believers.

They had accepted all the negativity in their lives and in their daily existence, believing it was the will of God. But I want to assure you today that there is no such thing as the will of God. When dealing with negative patterns in your life, people are suffering right before your eyes, and you say it's the will of God. God said No! It's not His will; it is the will of Satan. That is the lie from the pit of hell. What the Bible promises, it will be fulfilled in our lives. He will give our soul, spirit, and body satisfaction; we will be satisfied, as Paul said. Now, when you begin to see why your life is not aligning with what the Word of God says, know that the enemy is at work. As a Child of God, you have the power to command and reverse his action in the name of Jesus. The Bible says,

John 8:32 You will know the truth, and the truth will set you free.

And the truth is that when you are sure that you know there is an enemy, you begin to seek help. That's when you start looking for a deliverance ministry. If you are in a regular church, a church where you meet to drink coffee, eat muffins, and go home, know that your deliverance will take a little bit longer because deliverance is for only those who are truly desperate. The moment you leave that kind of church; the battle seems to start all over again. It's like you experience peace for just an hour while you're there, but as soon as you step outside, the fight picks right back up.

And there's no battle more exhausting; unlike spiritual battles, there is no painful battle like this spiritual battles. They are the most brutal battles that any man can face. That is why, when you are going through spiritual battles, you begin to seek deliverance ministries, fast, and pray, asking for God's guidance. Sometimes, God will prompt you to seek someone out you might even be led to go online. I've heard countless stories of people saying that as they searched for deliverance, one of my videos showed up right away, just when they needed it most. As they began watching and praying along with the video, they would start receiving their deliverance, sometimes even experiencing physical deliverance. So, we thank God for things like social media. Because God has been able to use some of the ministers, He has been able to extend His right arm and use these platforms for His glory in the mighty name of Jesus.

Now, back to the roots: when you begin to deal with the root, sometimes you don't know how deep the root you're dealing with is. It is easier to pull only one root, but if the root already has branches **(that means the forgotten generation, the forgotten foundation)**, the work here will need an extra layer of spiritual strength and authority to be able to uproot them through James 4:7. Submit to the Lord and resist the Devil, it shall flee from you, and also by having discipline with the things of God and consistency in pursuing the Lord through prayers, fasting, reading the word of God, and committing yourself fully to the Lord. In this case, you are the first generational commander meaning no one in the generations before you ever dealt with deliverance at the root. And now, that untouched root has grown branches, affecting many areas of life in the family line. In this case, it cannot be accomplished in a single act of deliverance. In every family, God will put a burden of deliverance on a person, a person who will begin to take the things of God very seriously, a person who will start to research why some of the things don't make sense in the family tree or bloodline; the one who will question if it is the will of God, and this person will jumpstart foundation deliverance by answering the call of God according to;

Isaiah 6:8: Also, I heard the voice of the Lord, saying, Whom shall I send, and who will go for us? Then said I, Here am I; send me.

This whole journey of deliverance, of course, is just to give us information that there are some abandoned matters in the foundations that the enemy is using to steal, kill, and destroy the family [John 10:10]. We walk through it with understanding, not in ignorance, just as our forefathers ignored the foundation completely. As you undergo deliverance, one of the primary actions you will repeatedly perform is confessing, repenting, renouncing, and asking for the cleansing of foundational sins, transgressions, and iniquities in the name of Jesus.

But the Bible says that **deliverance is the children's bread** (Matthew 15:26). Who are the children? The children are those who have received salvation through Jesus Christ. If you have not yet received Christ into your life or backslider, I invite you to do so now by praying this simple prayer for salvation so that you can gain the full benefit of what God is doing in this whole deep deliverance book; otherwise, we are going to be wasting Jesus' time here.

Salvation Prayer:

Heavenly Father, I come to You today just as I am. I confess that I am a sinner, and I ask You to forgive me. I believe that Jesus Christ is the Son of God, that He died for my sins, and that He rose again on the third day. Today, I choose to turn away from my old life and follow You. I invite You, Lord Jesus, to come into my heart and be my Lord and Savior. Fill me with Your Holy Spirit, and help me to live for You from this day forward. Thank you for saving me. In Jesus' name, Amen.

Now, as a child of God you are entitled to move to the next step which is; confessing, repenting, renouncing, and asking for the cleansing.

1. WHAT ARE YOU CONFESSING?
2. WHAT ARE YOU REPENTING?
3. WHAT ARE YOU RENOUNCING?
4. WHAT ARE YOU ASKING TO BE CLEANSED OF?

Confession and Renouncing of Sin in the 1st Generation, like Sorcery, Divination, Bloodshed, Adultery, Fornication, and Witchcraft. This is what birthed what you see manifesting in the 2nd generation as Transgression, because no one renounced or took any action to remove them.

Confession and Renunciation of Transgression in 2nd Generation: Rebellion, idolatry, bitterness, injustice, impurity, immorality, and greed. This is what birthed what you see manifesting in the 3rd generation as inequity, because no one renounced or took any action to remove them. In the 3rd generation they have turners to afflictions.

Asking for cleansing of inequity in the 3rd generation that brought afflictions like; madness, confusion, insanity, barrenness, poverty, slavery, infirmities, death, addiction, shame, reproach, oppression, vanity, blindness, rejection, demonic oppression, violence, abuse, sorrow, captivity, defilement, divorce, suicidal, homosexuality, polygamous witchcraft, masturbation, pornography, barrenness, depression, denial, limitation, spiritual blindness and premature death.

Foundational Deliverance is deep and detailed. If you tend to be partial in deliverance, you will leave some small roots unattended, and they will merge and grow again. Therefore, in our deliverance, we are mindful of this. Total and complete deliverance is a process; it's not quick, and it's not a one-day thing. Many, even vessels of God, have rejected deliverance. They are ministering to the sheep, yet they themselves are not delivered. Many who sit in church have attempted deliverance but never experienced complete freedom, due to a lack of knowledge. Instead, they have awakened deep spiritual troubles and demonic oppression because of **partial deliverance**. Others were once delivered but failed to maintain their deliverance again, because of a lack of knowledge.

In the bible we see the, case of Jehu, God anointed him to destroy the entire house of Ahab and Jezebel, but Jehu accidentally left Athaliah who is Jezebel's daughter, and that is how the wickedness from the house of Jezebel continued even after the death of Ahab and Jezebel.*2 Kings 11:1-12*

That's why the Bible says in James 4:7 **Submit to the Lord and resist the devil; it shall flee from you.** And this is how we take authority in Jeremiah 1:10, uproot, tear down, destroy, and then He said, '*overthrow.*'

How do you destroy?

And make sure that the root will never be on this face of the earth again by declaring:

Hebrews 12:29 My God is a consuming fire.

And command the uprooted to be set ablaze and burned to ashes and never again to manifest in my foundation, even to the unborn generation, in the name of Jesus. At this point, you have become the generation of John the Baptist. "*From the days of John the Baptist up until now, the Kingdom of our God suffered violence, and the violent take it by force.*" This is the point where you say, 'Enough is enough of what I'm seeing in my bloodline.' You take a bold stand to ensure the uprooting and deliverance of the captives of the mighty, as the Scripture says they shall all be delivered.

> **Isaiah 49:25: But thus says the LORD: "Even the captives of the mighty shall be taken away, and the prey of the terrible shall be delivered; for I will contend with him who contends with you, and I will save your children."**

We have the advantage of Jesus's blood, the power of the Cross, and the power of resurrection; we have all the weapons we need to wage war and win generational battles without becoming casualties through knowledge and understanding of warfare protocols and laws.

ERASE FOUNDATIONAL LAW AND WRITE NEW DIVINE LAW

The battle you see is a result of an active spiritual law at work. As you wage war as a commander, you take authority in the name of Jesus and erase all the spiritual laws ever written against you and your bloodline and your foundation with the blood of Jesus. Write another law and put a signature with the blood of Jesus; seal this law so that no one can ever go above it or attempt to erase it. Anyone who tries to undo what the Lord is doing in my foundation (rebuilding) will pay with their firstborn and lastborn according to Joshua in the bible. In other words, enough is enough of negative patterns, negative cycles, *enough of attacks of spirits and demons and Generational curses have to end with me.*

> *Joshua 6:26: At that time, Joshua pronounced this solemn oath: "Cursed before the Lord is the one who undertakes to rebuild this city, Jericho: 'At the cost of his firstborn son, he will lay its foundations; at the cost of his youngest, he will set up its gates."*

That's when you can be comfortable and confident that, at least for the first time, the root in your foundation is shaken. Now you can address the second part of Jeremiah 1:10, which involves building and planting, as the foundation has been cleared. You will start to see things slowly align as you plant and build through the authority in Jesus' name.

Deliverance can sometimes take a long time because most of us want to apply the second part of James 4:7: Resist the devil, and he will flee from you, but that is not always the case. God wants us to submit fully to Him first, so that He can help us with the foundational battles because it's not easy; you must first submit to God's will. You cannot resist the devil before that submission, for it is in submission that the breakthrough occurs; it is in submission that glory is found. In the submission, that's where the power of God is. Also, your deliverance will be quick and easy if the motives are right.

Foundational battles often have legal rights and active covenants in place, many of which people are unaware of. Without these covenants, Satan would have no access to a child of God. It is only God who can reveal these hidden covenants to us, so that we can deal with them effectively through the Word of God.

Also, keep in mind that no one can deliver you from foundational battles except God. I have heard powerful men and women of God openly admit that they avoid dealing with deliverance. Why? Because they understand how fierce and deeply rooted these foundational powers can be, they require time; this is not a one-touch deliverance that your church is used to, But again, I ask: Who then will deliver the children of God? Even if you choose not to engage in the deliverance of God's people, your church may be full, but it will be full of people in spiritual detention and chronic bondages. Numbers do not equal freedom. And if you yourself are truly delivered, you will not fear delivering others. Why? Because it is not you doing the work, it is God. That is why God commands that every servant must seek deliverance from Him if they truly desire to do His end-time work. For God to use you mightily, you must first be free.

Why do you want deliverance?

God does examine us on this. God wants you to be healed, delivered and restored, so that you can, in turn, give to others and deliver your foundation. The devil knows our motives and intentions; that's why he fights back-to-back to stop our progress and to disappoint us, to drain us with unending, intense daily battles. The Bible says in Matthew

7:24-27, *"The foolish builder built his house on the sand, and a wise man built his house on the rock."*

So now, this building is when you start to build as a wise man. Before that, you were building as a foolish man. That's why the wind kept coming and demolishing your Christ foundation, which you were building on top of the faulty foundation of your ancestors and not of Christ Jesus. However, after you have worked on Jeremiah 1:10, you are beginning to build and plant on the rock which is Christ Jesus.

It's a strong foundation. Strong base: You'll start to build on the rock that is now you. You are called a wise man, which, in other words, means that many of us were not wise men before because we were bypassing spiritual protocols and legal covenants that our forefathers put in place that were displeasing to God. That's why the enemy kept resisting us, denying us the right to serve Christ and enjoy Him. And I think our forefathers bypassed these four things (Jeremiah 1: 10 uproot, tear down, destroy, overthrow) because they require a lot of discipline and purity. When you begin to work on this scripture, the Lord will open your eyes. The Lord will start to show you through dreams and visions. The Lord will be showing you clearly as you are fasting and as you are praying. That's how I did mine.

The spiritual battle centers around five main kingdoms: the Marine Kingdom, the Witchcraft Kingdom, the Water Spirit Kingdom, the Serpentine Kingdom, and the Animal Kingdom. As long as these kingdoms remain active, they work to prevent anyone from fulfilling their God-given destiny. They will steal it, exchange it, kill it, destroy it. That is why God wants to work with you to make sure all these five kingdoms they are taken down in the name of Jesus. God is faithful and will reveal to you the spirit and the kingdom you still need to overcome, as well as the kind of kingdom you need to address. The reason God is showing you this is that you are ready, and He is entrusting you with the victory in the battle zone.

For deliverance to be complete, all five kingdoms must be addressed, because these kingdoms often work together. If you are delivered from only one, the others may still have access to your life, and it will seem as though you've escaped one trouble only to enter another. Which means there are still open satanic doors through these kingdoms, so, all have to be dealt with, and all open satanic doors, portals, altars have to be closed! No access, no fly zone.

What are those kingdoms?

1. Marine Kingdom

The concept of a "marine kingdom" or the "beast from the sea" in the Bible, particularly in the books of Daniel and Revelation, is often used symbolically to represent powerful, oppressive kingdoms or empires that arise from a state of chaos and disorder. In biblical imagery, the sea frequently symbolizes chaos, tumult, and rebellion against divine authority. These emerging kingdoms are portrayed as confusion, emerging from the sea, and resisting God's order. In Daniel 7, the prophet describes a vision of four great beasts rising from the sea, each symbolizing a dominant world empire that would rule over the earth and persecute God's people. These beasts serve as a prophetic representation of worldly powers that stand in opposition to God's kingdom, emphasizing the spiritual battle between divine authority and earthly rebellion.

What Are the Marine Spirits?

Even so, Leviathan and Python spirits are sometimes grouped under the broader category of "water spirits" or "marine spirits." Other names often associated with this class include Rahab, Merman, and Mermaid. According to some traditions, these so-called "marine spirits" are believed to dwell in water and are uncomfortable in dry environments. Jesus' reference to "dry places" in Luke 11:24 is sometimes cited as support for this belief. Additionally, the demons known as Legion, which Jesus cast out of a man living among the tombs, are considered by some to be marine spirits because they entered a herd of pigs that then rushed into the sea (Luke 8:26–33). In this lore, a marine spirit may also manifest as a succubus or incubus, forming a "spiritual spouse" relationship with a person. These entities are sometimes referred to as "husband spirits" or "wife spirits" and are believed to promote sexual lust and perversion. However, the true remedy for lust, fornication and other persistent sins is not found in rebuking so-called marine spirits, but in prayer, discipleship, and humble submission to God (James 4:7). It is of no use to blame mermaids, converse with evil spirits, or construct new mythologies victory comes through faith, obedience, and the transforming power of the Holy Spirit.

Dream:

Dreaming that you are breastfeeding strange children while experiencing barrenness in real life, or finding yourself pregnant in a dream despite chronic infertility, may indicate spiritual manipulation. Such dreams can signify the work of the marine kingdom or familiar spirits, aiming to counterfeit or steal your blessings. Likewise, dreams involving sexual intercourse, whether with unfamiliar or familiar individuals, can represent demonic activity where spiritual agents collect sperm or reproductive essence and take it to satanic laboratories to produce demonic offspring.

Other troubling dreams, such as giving money to strangers or acquaintances, often symbolize the loss or transfer of financial virtue. Seeing a twin or substitute in a dream may represent a demonic spirit sent to steal your blessings just before they manifest. These types of dreams often precede real-life symptoms such as miscarried miracles, repeated failure at the edge of breakthrough, and persistent disappointment. All of these point to spiritual oppression, particularly from marine powers and familiar spirits. Such dreams serve as a warning and a call to engage in focused prayer, spiritual warfare, and deliverance to reclaim what has been stolen and to break the cycle of delay and defeat.

Prayer Points:

1. Abba Father, I come before You in the name of Jesus, asking for deliverance from every marine spirit initiation over my life and my family, in the name of Jesus.

2. By the authority in the name of Jesus, I break every covenant made knowingly or unknowingly with marine spirits, in Jesus' name.

3. Father, in the name of Jesus, by Your power, I uproot every influence of the marine kingdom over my finances, generational wealth, and generational birthright, in Jesus' name.

4. By the power and authority in the name of Jesus, I cancel and destroy every marine spirit altar raised against me by the blood of Jesus.

5. My Father and my God, send Your warrior angels to fight on my behalf against every marine spirit, in the name of Jesus.

2. Water Spirit Kingdom

Water spirits are supernatural beings associated with bodies of water, including rivers, lakes, and oceans. Found in various cultures and folklore, they are often portrayed as shapeshifters, sometimes benevolent and sometimes malevolent, and may appear in many forms, including humans, mermaids, animals, or sea monsters like Leviathan. In the Bible, Leviathan is depicted as a powerful sea creature symbolizing chaos and evil. Psalm 74:14 describes God crushing Leviathan and giving it as food to the creatures of the wilderness.

Isaiah 27:1 speaks of God punishing and slaying Leviathan, the twisting serpent, while Job 41 offers a detailed description emphasizing its immense strength and fearsome nature. It represents evil forces that seek to oppose or hinder God's people. The Bible consistently warns against worshipping false gods and being deceived by evil spirits, including those linked to water. Believers are urged to remain vigilant, reject evil influences, and instead seek the power, guidance, and protection of the Holy Spirit.

Dream:

Dreaming that you are always around water bodies can be a spiritual indication that your treasures, such as blessings, virtues, gifts, talents, or even marriage, have been stolen, exchanged, or hidden in or under the water. Such dreams may indicate spiritual bondage linked to marine powers or ancestral dedications to water spirits. In some cases, it suggests that a person was unknowingly dedicated to the waters through family covenants or rituals. These dreams should not be ignored; they require intense spiritual warfare through prayer, fasting, and the declaration of God's Word. You must rise in faith to pursue, overtake, and recover all that has been stolen from you. Through the power and authority of Jesus Christ, you can reclaim your destiny, break ungodly covenants, and restore what the enemy has taken.

Prayer Points:

1. My Father and my God, I ask You to remove every curse and the resulting fruits in my life that came from my ancestors' and my own involvement with water spirits, in the name of Jesus Christ.

2. My God and my King, please remove all curses placed upon my ancestral family as a result of their evil associations and involvement with water spirits, in the name of Jesus Christ.

3. By the authority in the blood of Jesus, I break and cancel every spell, hex, enchantment, bewitchment, and incantation that has come upon me through my involvement with evil associations, water spirits, and ancestral spirits, in the name of Jesus Christ.

4. By the authority in the name of Jesus, I break and revoke every blood covenant, soul-tie, siege, and yoke connected to water spirits in my life, in the name of Jesus Christ.

5. Lord, I ask You to remove from my habits, thoughts, will, emotions, and body everything that has caused me to walk under the influence of water spirits and any other related spirits, in the name of Jesus Christ."

3. Serpentine Kingdom

The Concept of Serpentine Spirits in a Spiritual Context

In a spiritual context, serpentine spirits often refer to dark or negative forces associated with serpents. These spirits are typically seen as agents of deception and evil, working against the purposes of God. The Bible often employs serpentine imagery to represent forces of deceit, most notably in the account of the Fall of Man.

Genesis 3:1 states: "Now the serpent was craftier than any beast of the field which the LORD God had made. And he said to the woman, 'Indeed, has God said. This passage introduces the serpent as a symbol of cunning and deceit, ultimately leading Adam and Eve into sin by distorting God's word.

Similarly, in Acts 16:16, we read: "And it came to pass, as we went to prayer, a certain girl, having a pythonical spirit, met us, who brought her masters much gain by divining." This passage describes a young girl possessed by a spirit of divination, sometimes interpreted as a "python spirit", which is linked to serpentine influence and occult practices. The spirit was not only deceptive but also profitable to her handlers, as it provided false spiritual insights.

Serpentine spirits are commonly associated with harmful traits such as deceit, spiritual darkness, and destruction. They are seen as forces that lead individuals away from God, truth, and righteous living. In many spiritual traditions, these spirits are connected with death, the unknown, and the perversion of divine truth.

Due to their deceptive nature, serpentine spirits are often regarded as spiritual adversaries. Believers are encouraged to overcome these influences through prayer, spiritual discernment, and adherence to God's Word. The battle against such spirits is framed as part of the broader spiritual warfare described in Scripture, a conflict between good and evil, light and darkness.

In summary, serpentine spirits represent deceptive and destructive forces that work against spiritual growth and truth. The Bible presents these spirits as enemies to be resisted through faith, prayer, and obedience to God. Recognizing their influence is the first step in overcoming them and walking in the freedom that Christ offers.

Dreams:

In the serpentine kingdom, individuals may experience dreams involving serpents or even encounter spiritual or physical manifestations of snakes in their environment. These serpent powers often signify ancestral or generational strongholds, particularly when there is a history of serpent worship or occult practices in the family line, commonly referred to as the "father's house." Such dreams or encounters may indicate that covenants made in the past are still active and have not yet been broken through deliverance. Without seeking spiritual freedom and renouncing these covenants, these powers may continue to exert influence. These experiences serve as a warning and a call to pursue deliverance, prayer, and a deeper alignment with Christ's authority.

Prayer Points

1. My God, Mighty One in battle, I confess, renounce, and repent of any association with the serpentine kingdom. I ask that every covenant be broken by the blood of Jesus, and that You cleanse me and my family, in the name of Jesus.

2. O God, I ask that Your mighty hand and the great sword of fire destroy every serpent spirit dwelling in me, my family, and our environment, tormenting us in the name of Jesus.

3. I command the serpentine kingdom and every serpentine spirit troubling me: by the authority in the name of Jesus, swallow your own venom and every affliction you have released, now, in the name of Jesus.

4. By the authority in the name of Jesus, I release the Lord's sword of fire to cut the serpent into pieces, pierce its neck of strength, shatter its shield of scales, and sever its lengthy tail, in the name of Jesus.

5. Now, I take charge over my foundation. I reclaim my throne and repossess the Garden of Eden of my destiny, through the blood of Jesus.

4. Witchcraft Kingdom

The Concept of a Witchcraft Kingdom

The term "witchcraft kingdom" often refers to a realm of influence, power, or activity associated with witchcraft, magic, and the occult. It is commonly understood as a spiritual domain that exists beyond the physical world, an unseen realm where magic, spirits, and supernatural forces are believed to operate. This realm exalts itself against the knowledge of God, directly opposing His truth and righteousness.

According to Scripture, God views witchcraft and all related practices, such as divination, sorcery, and occultism, as abominations. In Deuteronomy 18:9–15, God gives clear warnings to His people not to imitate the detestable practices of other nations, which include witchcraft and consulting with the dead. These actions are spiritually corrupt and lead people away from the knowledge and worship of the true God.

Galatians 5:20 lists witchcraft among the works of the flesh, which are in opposition to the fruit of the Spirit. The Bible teaches that such practices are sinful and lead to separation from God. In 2 Corinthians 10:5, Paul urges believers to "demolish arguments and every pretension that sets itself up against the knowledge of God, and take captive every thought to make it obedient to Christ." This is a call to spiritual warfare, resisting every influence that contradicts God's Word and submitting our minds fully to Christ.

God's stance on wickedness is clear: He hates sin with a perfect hatred. Isaiah 48:22 and Isaiah 57:21 declare that "there is no peace for the wicked." Those who choose to follow the path of rebellion and unrighteousness will not experience the peace and blessings that God offers to those who walk in His ways.

In conclusion, the "witchcraft kingdom" represents a domain that stands in opposition to God's kingdom. It is a counterfeit power, one that seeks to deceive and destroy. But God, in His righteousness and holiness, calls His people to reject such practices and to pursue truth, obedience, and spiritual purity through Christ.

Dreams:

People affected by the influence of the witchcraft kingdom often experience troubling dreams, such as eating in a dream, having sex in a dream, being chased, finding themselves in graveyards or forests, attending strange or unfamiliar meetings, or revisiting former places, houses, or old friendships. Other common symbols include appearing in dreams without shoes or clothing, which can represent vulnerability, shame, or spiritual attack. These types of dreams are not to be taken lightly; they serve as a call to prayer, spiritual discernment, and a reminder to stand firm in faith and exercise authority through Christ. Recognizing the spiritual significance of these dreams is the first step toward deliverance and victory in the spiritual realm.

Prayer Points:

1. By the authority in the name of Jesus, any blood reorienting me and my family on any witchcraft altar I reject you, I renounce you. I command the sacrifice to dry up, and I command the altar to be demolished, in the name of Jesus.

2. Every covenant with the witchcraft kingdom within my life, my family tree, and my foundation breaks now by the power in the blood of Jesus.

3. By the authority in the name of Jesus, I command every satanic satellite, mirror, and computer monitoring my God-given destiny, and every satanic database collecting information from my ancestors, to shatter into irretrievable pieces now, in the name of Jesus.

4. I announce that every monitoring spirit and anything planted in my body or surroundings by evil and unreasonable men intended to monitor my progress must catch fire and burn to ashes, in the name of Jesus.

5. Any witchcraft exchange done in my life or body, be reversed by fire, in the name of Jesus.

5. Animal Kingdom

When people experience animals chasing them in dreams, it is often interpreted as a sign that dark powers are being released against them on a spiritual battlefield. Such dreams may indicate an intensifying spiritual conflict, but they can also be a sign of spiritual progress. Satan does not waste his weapons on those who pose no threat. If you are being attacked, it may mean you are advancing spiritually and becoming a target because you are winning.

Dreams:

In dream symbolism, different animals can represent specific spiritual issues or attacks: dogs often symbolize lust, lions represent fear, tigers indicate aggression, bulls are associated with foundational powers or ancestral strongholds, and alligators may suggest hidden dangers or predatory threats. Goats are commonly linked with stubbornness, rebellion, or spiritual contamination. These dreams serve as a call to prayer, spiritual discernment, and a reminder to stand firm in faith and authority through Christ.

Prayer Points:

1. Abba Father, I thank You for Your protection over my life and my family. Let your divine covering shield us from every unclean spirit manifesting through the animal kingdom, in the name of Jesus.

2. My God, Mighty Man of War who never loses a battle, by Your power, scatter every plan of the enemy represented by unclean animals in my dreams or surroundings, in the name of Jesus.

3. By the authority in the name of Jesus, I plead the blood of Jesus over my household and declare that no unclean spirit shall gain access to my life or my family, in Jesus' name.

4. Lion of Judah, mighty in battle, Father, release Your warring angels to surround me as I pray this midnight prayer against unclean animals, in the name of Jesus.

5. My God, King of kings and Lord of lords, let Your fire destroy every unclean animal representing demonic oppression in my life and in my family, in the name of Jesus.

Luke 10:19: Behold, I give you power to tread on serpents and scorpions, and over all the power of the enemy: and nothing shall hurt you by any means.

You continue to fight, pray, and fast. When it is clear that the spirit, power, demon, or stronghold has been dealt with, most of the time, dreams will change, visions will change, sickness will disappear, and disorders will be addressed. Also, if the matter were a spirit spouse from water spirits, you would not see it again. That means you have been delivered from that kingdom.

Additionally, the Lord will cease showing you the kingdom He previously revealed and instead show you another kingdom that remains, allowing you to begin dealing with a different realm, such as a witchcraft kingdom, a serpentine or a marine entity. You will begin to deal with one kingdom after another; that is when you start to experience breakthroughs of the things that Satan has long withheld; for example, finances will begin to flow, disorders will begin to depart, dreams will change, spirit spouses will leave, and witchcraft feeding you in dreams will start to disappear. Once these kingdoms are broken and gone, you'll experience greater ease in your prayer life and true freedom in your faith journey. The enemy will no longer strike you with headaches that prevent you from reading the Word, and you will be able to fast even more than you did before. And that is how chronic disease will disappear from you once and for all.

Chronic infirmity, sickness and disease connected to the dark kingdom are designed to keep you continually spending money on pharmaceuticals; this is referred to as Pharmakeia, when you become aggressive on them by warfare prayers and fasting, that is how they leave you, because the body the environment is not conducive for them to lodge any longer and that is your deliverance.

Many of these kingdoms don't just give up easily; they will often retaliate. For example, witchcraft will create a night catering service where they feed you in the dream to reinitiate you, and the reason is that they know they can capture every single part of your destiny and the destinies of your people. Generational good health has been captured in the hands of Satan, who has traded them on the satanic market, which is why you find some diseases running from generation to generation. Divorce from generation to generation. So, Satan has made himself comfortable from past generations; they have captured everything. Now, if they find one knowledgeable person like you who understands that life is spiritual, you can begin to take the right stand and fight them by uprooting them through the weapon of the word of God, the blood of Jesus and the name Jesus.

The enemy doesn't like people with spiritual understanding; the enemy is comfortable with spiritually ignorant people. Spiritually knowledgeable people seek the truth; they don't settle for less because the Bible says, '*You shall know the truth, and the truth shall set you free.*'

So now, when you begin to search, you will know, and the more you know, the more you will recover.

Jeremiah 33:3 Call to me, and I will answer you and will tell you great and hidden things that you have not known.

The powers of your father's house are starting to deal with you; now they're hunting your life. They must ensure that they take you down because they know you have discovered the secret, and you are about to unseat them from their throne, which they have stolen from generation to generation. The Lord has uncovered the hidden secret.

You were blind, but now you see; you are beginning to inquire from the Lord, and the Lord is showing you. You will be the first person to uproot them and clear your foundation. They don't want anyone like you. They want those who are ignorant. those who take things easy. They don't want those who are asking why and how this negative issue persists? 'Why is this negative information still there, e.g., premature death, suicidal?' Why is this problem still there, e.g., infirmity? What is the cause of this financial crisis? When they regard you as a threat to their kingdom, they will work hard to reinitiate you so that you don't escape their kingdom.

Re-initiation often involves paralysing your prayer life, quenching your spiritual fire, and causing severe migraine headaches that force you to sleep and rest instead of praying and worshipping God. It may also include mental attacks and feelings of anger toward God.

Initiation is often experienced in dreams, whether through feeding or sexual means. That's when you see an increase in feeding in dreams, sex and rape in dreams, dream criminals attacks increases all is done in the dream to reinitiate you by force. As you grow stronger in prayer and deepen your spiritual strength, your inner man becomes more powerful. Over time, you'll gain the ability to overcome eating and sexual dreams. They may still come, but you'll recognize them and confront them right within the dream. The journey of deliverance is truly both a challenge and a battle. If you haven't started your deliverance, you haven't started the real foundational battle. It's a battle they don't want to let go of, and they have been holding on to everything for many years. Remember, when you are delivered, it's not only for you; it's for your entire bloodline.

God needs one whom He will use to deliver His people. When you receive the deliverance, it's intended for anyone connected to your bloodline, anyone related to you by DNA, which is why the enemy is angry. This is why the devil is angry, because you are depopulating hell.

In other words, they have taken all the generations, even the unborn. You may have children who are misbehaving, disobedient, and rebellious, and this is because they have already been taken; they are under satanic manipulation and control, evil projection; they are under monitoring spirits and astral projection, That is why every believer must cut the silver cord of astral projection every day that no one can project into you life.

That's why you see young children suffering from ADHD, slow development, cerebral palsy, Down Syndrome and autism. This is because they already have their souls in prison in captivity, their souls have been traded to the satanic market, so they are planting satanic seeds, and these souls function at their command until someone rises to cry for these souls to be set free, In the name of Jesus.

These powers of darkness will fight anyone who discovers them and seeks to eliminate them. The Bible says in *2 Thessalonians 2:7,For the secret power of lawlessness is already at work; but the one who now holds it back will continue to do so till he is taken out of the way.*

Powers of darkness in the foundation know clearly that this is their last option; the territory is being captured, taken away, and returned to its original owner, who is the Child of God. God will show you exactly what's going on; you are not alone in this generational battle. The reason God is showing you this is that you are the one who is the engineer. He will take you through the details of this process to make sure no root shall be left unuprooted. God has given you the capacity, capability, wisdom, weapons, and all the strength you need for these special tasks. You cannot be a casualty; you will surely come out victorious.

This is not the time to say, "I've prayed," and then just go to sleep. No, this is the time to watch and pray. Ask: What is the condition and position of the enemy? God will reveal it all to you through dreams and visions. And if the enemy is still active, you go after them again relentlessly until they fully surrender to the power of your God, the Lord Jesus Christ of Nazareth.

Remember the plagues of Egypt? It was God himself who fought through all for the Israelites. But do you know why Pharaoh was so stubborn? It is the same process you are experiencing; the enemy will not give up immediately, and even after giving up, will still pursue you to see if you still have the strength to fight him again. That is why even after our rescue, we don't stop fighting; we don't go back to sleep. Your inner self must always be strong and alert, "watch and pray at all times."

You are good if God is with you. The dark kingdom remains in place and continues to operate, still fighting to retain its territory. They will gang up and retaliate. When you see them initiating you through dreams, fight back. This does not mean you are failing or losing. No! They are contending because they know their time is over; they continue fighting, for God is with you, and the battle is the Lord's.

How do you continue fighting?

We have created numerous resources to help you navigate these challenges. Find time to pray with these videos every day as the enemy intensifies; pray according to the things God has shown you through these videos; fight one kingdom after another. Especially if your foundation has not been touched in terms of deliverance, it is also possible that it is not only one kingdom that is against you.

It's a process one kingdom at a time will fall. As you may think you are fighting the witchcraft kingdom, you begin to dream about snakes, start to dream about spirit spouses, and start to dream that you are in water bodies. You may even begin to dream of recovering your treasure box from the marine kingdom that's a sign of victory. But before you started pursuing foundational deliverance, these kingdoms had never appeared and never manifested until you made up your mind to begin the journey of the family tree and foundational deliverance.

In the journey of deliverance, Satan fears the one who is serious and knows what to do. That is when he dispatches his greatest weapons from the five kingdoms to attack and potentially stop that person. Satan does not waste his most powerful weapons on someone who is not a threat to his kingdom.

You also need to understand that Satan is not bothered if you're not confronting him or threatening his kingdom. In fact, he's perfectly fine with you being a lukewarm believer.

Living in, normalizing, or even legalizing sin such as fornication, lying, unlawful relationships, unholy marriages, having children outside of wedlock, idolatry, drinking, drug use, partying or clubbing, and surrounding yourself with ungodly influences while still attending church and reading the Bible, is a dangerous contradiction. It is a deception that hinders genuine spiritual growth and intimacy with God.

Even if you're showing up in church and opening your Bible, holding onto these sinful practices keeps the hand of God far from your life. These are not just lifestyle choices—they are spiritual traps, often rooted in satanic influence, designed to keep you from walking in true holiness and power.

Satan is fine with that; he won't waste his weapons to fight you because he knows you are already aligned with his agenda. But the moment you become serious with God and seek true deliverance, Satan will begin to reveal that your affliction runs deeper than you thought that you are entangled with all five kingdoms, both in your life and in your bloodline.

Deliverance is a journey; it is a process, and it's not quick. If you know you're in a hurry, forget about true deep deliverance; if you know you need a quick fix, there nothing like that just you know. Anyone who is promising anything like that to you is deceiving you and setting you up for more traps.

Deliverance is the children's bread, Jesus said, and not for popcorn believers. That is why anyone, whether a man or a woman of God or just a regular person who has undergone deliverance, is cautious about sin. The reason is that deliverance is time consuming and demands a high level of purity, holiness, righteousness, obedience and constant deep consecration. Now, if you have invested all this, do you think you will allow sin easily? That is not possible; I like it when I meet people who are delivered. One thing I can tell you is that they are cautious with everything: with the environment, the kind of circle they allow themselves to be in, the food they eat, and where to go and where not to go. Be cautious with everything because the world we live in is so cunning, and the Bible tells us not to be ignorant of the schemes of the crafty.

Chapter 3:
How to Intensify Your Deliverance?

You don't need to have one-on-one deliverance; what you need is time. Regardless of your busy schedule, you must make sure to watch a video on deliverance or warfare at least once a day. In this case, you may not see immediate results in the physical realm, but in the spiritual realm, you are advancing and making progress; the fire is intensifying, and all the spirits, demons can't survive the fire. Now, what remains is the stronghold. But through consistency and disciplined pursuit of the things of God, you send a clear and bold message not just to hell, but also to Heaven that you're serious about walking in victory and fulfilling your purpose. At this point, God knows that my son or my daughter is earnest, and Satan also knows this and that they are about to lose territory.

I have many people testifying, including those who have listened to the previous prayers on the video regarding specific issues of deliverance. The Lord has told us, in Psalms 107:20, that *He sent out His word and healed them all, delivered them all.* God is trying to make our job easier. So, when you listen to the Holy Spirit, the Spirit of God will guide you in choosing the video that will deliver you. Our deliverance videos are available on all major platforms and are free to access.

> *Matthew 9:37: Then saith he unto his disciples, the harvest truly is plenteous, but the laborers are few.*

God is in the business of choosing and using His own in a tremendous way that no man can understand. God is at a point of proving His word, that He will use the foolish things of this world to shame the wise. God is amplifying the voice of the vessel He chooses to use, and no man, demon, spirit, power of hell, nor any personality can stop what God is doing right now. That's how I accepted the work of God, even though I didn't know how these things were done. The Spirit of the living God is truly faithful a constant teacher who has taught me and continues to guide me every step of the way. I thank the Spirit of God for His guidance. I thank him for choosing this broken vessel and displaying it through deliverance for His glory.

You will be certain that you have been delivered if you stop seeing Kingdoms in the dream. For example, dogs are associated with the spirit of lust, snakes represent the spirit of divination and the serpentine kingdom, and dead relatives are familiar spirits. What does this mean? It means that the kingdom that you still see in the dream or vision is the one in control of your life. Remember, life is deeply spiritual. What you see in your dreams reflects activity in the spirit realm that's your true reality. If the satanic kingdom is controlling your spiritual life, it means they hold the remote control, dictating the course of your life. And as long as they remain active, they will continue to manipulate and interfere with your destiny. You must fight for your deliverance and ensure that the spiritual remote control of your life is snatched from the enemy's hands and returned to your own; that's what we call total and complete deliverance.

And what I'm telling you is that I'm a living testimony. What I know now, I wish I had known ten years ago. I also wish churches would take the subject of deliverance more seriously and teach people the truth about it, rather than remaining silent about deliverance and leaving people bound by various kinds of bondage. Allow people to seek their deliverance. I am very sure that a delivered pastor would love all his congregation to be delivered and set free. That is the character of a person who has been delivered and set free. If anyone denies his members' deliverance, that means he has not been delivered.

In many churches I have visited, I was assured that Jesus had finished it all, but only to find that the more I believed Jesus had finished it all, the more my battles advanced, because a faulty foundation had not been addressed. In church, nobody discussed foundational battles; nobody spoke about deliverance. Nobody was ready to begin the journey of truth. No man of God could help me; the help of prayer was just temporary, but the real battle was still ongoing. At some point, I felt like even God was not helping me. This is the case for many. Many are fighting silent battles; many don't want to speak about it. This includes many men of God on the pulpit who have not been delivered.

They have decided to leave that portion alone as if it doesn't concern them. However, the truth is that deliverance requires a high level of discipline in terms of purity and consistency. Because of this, many decide to pass on deliverance and ignore the foundational matters; nobody pays attention to them, regardless of the afflictions in their lives. Until God hears the cry for deliverance, He chooses someone and sends them to deliver people; these are the ones called by the Lord. They are His chosen vessels, and when they respond, they begin to listen closely to the Holy Spirit and follow His lead. Through them, the Lord starts to move powerfully in their families, churches, and foundations, restoring what the enemy has wasted: The enemy has wasted time, seasons, destinies, and even entire bloodlines.

So, deliverance, Jesus said, is the children's bread; we have sought this knowledge and pursued deliverance. Once you do this, the element that has wasted your life begins to fade away slowly, and all the promises of God begin to come to fruition; also, the disorders start to disappear and the heavenly governmental order of God comes into alignment.

But the point now is, if the foundations are destroyed, what can a righteous person do? Therefore, every righteous person must return and repair the damaged foundation. The foundation now becomes even more confused when they realize you are one of their own, yet you belong to Jesus, you are Jesus' advocate. It's like you throw them into confusion suddenly, they begin to fight back. At this stage, it becomes a matter of power versus power. That's why it's crucial to be spiritually prepared and confident in what you're doing before you bring the name of Jesus into the battle. Make sure there's no legal grounds in your foundation that they can use against you, because they will look for it especially from the satanic database of your foundation. I must be the one to bring fire on them because my time has come; I now know the truth, and I am so determined that this time I must be set free and my foundation must be delivered and be brought back to the Kingdom of God.

Powers of darkness that have been holding me, they have to lose the ground that they made like brass for me, lose my territory so the Spirit of God can take over, for the child of God has arisen; the amazing grace of God has located me, my family, and my generation, we were blind but now we see.

If amazing grace has found me, I was blind but now I see, my job is to ensure that deliverance and freedom are established in my foundation by uprooting the evil roots that were still there; in that way, you don't want to be like the foolish man who built his house on the sand. You begin to build and plant on the foundation that has been liberated and is free from any satanic connection. Jesus says, *'Upon this rock I shall build my church, and the gates of hell shall not prevail.'*

Now you can boldly call yourself a born-again child of God, because you're building your life on a solid, unshakable foundation. And now that you know the truth, remember the Bible says it's the truth that sets you free, in the name of Jesus.

Many believers have yet to discover the truth. That is why they claim the name of Jesus but show no evidence of freedom sitting in church, bound by spiritual chains, reading their Bibles while still in bondage. It is the truth that sets one free. If you have not accepted the truth you will stay in this bondage forever.

War Against Powers of Darkness

In the Book of Ephesians 6:12, the Bible says, *For we wrestle not against flesh and blood, but against principalities, against powers, against the rulers of darkness of this world. Against spiritual wickedness in high places.*

In the scripture above, you see spiritual battles. It's the reality that someone can't express because it is complicated. Spiritual battles are often deeply personal they're the kind of struggles no one else can truly see or understand. Even if you have a husband or a wife, they may not fully grasp what you're going through. It's your battle, between you and God, and it's something only you can fight through with His strength. That's why it can easily lead you to depression, suicidal thoughts, isolation, moodiness, and suspiciousness. No one can understand spiritual battles for you. You can be a father if your child is going through spiritual battles you can't see; you can't help because you don't understand.

Unless you are a person who walks in the supernatural, connected to the spirit of the living God, staying close to God is how He will reveal and disclose to you the hidden secrets of the enemy, as you draw near to Him through prayer, fasting, and consecration. Many are the times when these battles manifest in our children or our family members as afflictions (disobedience, libel, isolation, suicidal tendencies, stiff neck, failing in schools, anger, rejection, obesity, addiction etc.). That's why the Bible says we wrestle not against flesh and blood.

"Life is spiritual, and it is an unending battle because the kingdom of darkness underestimated the children of God regarding the things of the Spirit. Physical battles that you can see are easier than spiritual. You see the gun; you know the war, but the spiritual battle is another thing that will keep you in bondage, leaving you unsure of what to do or how to proceed. However, we thank God that these days, there are many solutions. You need to understand more about spiritual battles and how to help yourself and your family members because you are the answer for this generation. You can experience deliverance on your own just by listening to teachings on deliverance and participating. So, as children of God, if you are failing to seek deliverance, it means you are not serious about your deliverance, because the knowledge is readily available, the materials are accessible; it is simply a matter of you and your time.

Deliverance is hard work, and it is more profound, especially if you are a first-generation commander or a leader; you cannot expect someone to do everything for you. You can pray that God will put someone close to you for guidance. They interpret your dreams and advise you to pray specific prayers; some may even suggest fasting, depending on the dream and what the person feels led by the Holy Spirit to do. Spiritual battles require you to embark on this journey and wage war after putting on the full armour of God and the whole armour of light, because it is a very tough endeavour. Now, when you begin to seek deep deliverance from profound bondages, you will understand that there are more hidden things; the minute you start to touch on deliverance, it's as if all hell breaks loose upon you. You may start having multiple dreams at once and that's a clear sign of just how faulty your foundation is. It's the spirit realm revealing the depth of what needs to be addressed, delivered and healed.

God, in His mercy, is trying to show you that nothing has been worked on, so start working and take the journey of deliverance very seriously. God is showing you that there are powers in the foundation that are speaking against what you are about to do, pursuing total and complete deliverance. There are ancient altars that have legal rights. Altars and covenants have been in place for ages and have remained untouched. So, when you begin to touch them, all hell breaks loose.

Some believers in influential churches often overlook an essential problem: the issue with such churches is that the anointing of a powerful man or woman of God often covers them. You have not been delivered; you are just covered or protected for a moment. That's why you find that when such people leave that church or that coverage, all hell breaks loose again because you were not delivered; you were walking under somebody's anointing, and they never even told you to work on your deliverance because they want to keep you enslaved. They don't usually teach about deliverance or reveal secrets about it; instead, they have you believe that you are delivered because you fell under the anointing and you are under the leadership of a powerful man or woman of God.

They want always to keep you dependent on them, which I find weird because the Bible says *the harvest is plentiful, but the workers are few*. I feel that the anointing the Lord has placed on me is to distribute this material and knowledge to each person, so that many can work on their deliverance and be set free, allowing the Lord to use them in His vineyard. Remember, before you are delivered, you cannot be fully utilized, or you will be limited to what information God can reveal to you. Because what happens when you are delivered fully? God can trust you and give you the secret of the Kingdom, along with all the necessary weapons to conquer the enemy in battle. All the essential weapons you need, all the vital support you require, whether financial wisdom or knowledge, anything you need, God will release to you when you are entirely and ultimately delivered.

So, if you're not fully and completely delivered, imagine God releasing His blessings and wealth over you those lingering powers still attached to your life will try to strip it all away. They'll steal what God intended for you, because the legal ground hasn't yet been broken and removed.

That's why God has given me an assignment to deliver and spread this message. This is revival; let as many people be delivered. If I am to be a vessel God will use to deliver them by the grace of God, or if they have to do it on their own, I have to stress this to people so that they understand the importance of deliverance, that they can come clean and be ready to be used entirely by God.

If you are not willing to be fully delivered, you can't tap into the full glory of God or your God-given destiny. The spiritual legal rights that are still in place are denying you rights as a child of God. The Bible said that Joshua, a high priest, still had a filthy garment on him, and Satan was standing right there to accuse him and deny him what God was releasing to him. That's why you hear me insisting on deliverance to the people of God. Work on your deliverance. Make sure it is complete so when being used to bring deliverance to other people, Satan will not accuse you with your filthy garment if you are not delivered yet. That's why you must have understood don't walk in ignorance, declaring, "I'm a man of God," while wearing filthy garments in the spirit. We have to take deliverance seriously. Without it, we can't fully walk in what God has given us. The enemy will keep finding ways to steal, kill, and destroy as long as there's an open door in our lives.

As long as there is access, they can cause harm to you because they perceive you as a threat to their kingdom and themselves. Make sure you walk in the full coverage of the blood of Jesus and the whole armor of God, which includes the helmet of salvation, the breastplate of righteousness, the belt of truth, the sandals of the gospel of peace, the shield of faith, and the sword of the Spirit. Don't stay ignorantly thinking that all is well. Once you touch the Kingdom of Darkness, deliverance from deep battles comes with repercussions and backlash. So, stay understanding as you begin this journey; you must always remain vigilant. You must be ready; the Bible says, *'I have made you a watchman over the walls of Jerusalem.'* Now, how can you be a watchman and choose times? A watchman is on duty at his assigned post all the time.

During my deliverance process, I encountered significant turbulence and battles because, initially, they would resist me, thinking I might give up. However, I was determined because I knew that one of us would surrender in the end, and that was not my portion. As you continue to engage, they begin to lose the battle. Now you enter the cruise line, where you don't have to fight in the warfare zone, in dreams, or visions, because you are in control. Even if you feel a release in your spirit, don't rest; keep fighting, even though there is no warfare; keep doing the same thing every day. Why? Because they are hiding, you can go back to sleep, thinking that you have been delivered, and then they can come back like a flood.

That is why you should remain in your post of assignment in this case, which is prayer. Many kingdoms are already leaving, but foundational strongmen and strongholds are challenging to get rid of. That is why you shouldn't leave your post, no matter how much release you feel. Those strongmen and strongholds are the agents of hell in your family; they are priests and prophetesses. They continue to nourish the faulty foundation by empowering corrupt legal covenants, thereby keeping them alive, active and in place. They are sacrificing to them; they have that assignment to continually feed them daily, monthly, or yearly, depending on the covenant. We still have some tribes and religions in my country that go to visit the villages yearly, where they perform rituals in the graveyard where their loved ones, grandfathers, or fathers are buried, and they engage in various activities, including prayers, eating and drinking, among others. I believe many people are unaware, but the family priestess is privy to all the sacrifices they make to their gods each year; it's a covenant in place and a graveyard spirit, the spirit of the dead that controls that family.

People make these sacrifices, and many don't know what they are doing; they just follow. We have some who are ignorant- they're doing that, and they don't know the implications.

However, some of them recognise that they are nurturing the covenant because there must be someone who will continually make sacrifices; they pass the button or the septal from generation to generation, at least to one member of the family who is committed to doing so. **Satan is so clever, and he has ruled your family forever. Even if you chase him out now, he still has to leave a representative at least one. Satan is not ready to surrender all; it is a battle. This battle belongs to God.**

These covenants can be so profound and brutal, depending on the power of your clan with these gods. No matter how robust your tribe was or is, some of them require human flesh and blood. In such places, there's usually a prevalence of deaths by accident or disease, kidnapping, and loss of children. Where did the children go? They have been sacrificed. The more these principalities feel threatened by your presence, the more they must demand even greater sacrifices. Many children of God are beginning to understand that these daily sacrifices are the sources of their captivity, pain, disappointment and failures. This is to ensure they remain even stronger, maintaining control.

If they can't get enough blood, they will attack pregnant women- that is, if there are pregnant women around the clan or tribe, which means a regular occurrence of pregnant women losing their pregnancies. I was one of them, my seed, my pregnancy was fought, too. But God, in His mercy, had a purpose for my life. He has designed my life in such a way that I fight hard battles and escape without a scar. That is because I stood up at this stage as much as I did and said, *'No! this far and no farther. I demand a pure generation; my womb shall be a representation of heaven, and my seed shall be a seed of a pure generation. Satan is forbidden now and forever to lay dirty hands on this seed, the fruit of my womb. From now on, this must be clean bloodlines; it should be a clean generation that God will be pleased of this human creation.*

I had to put on my armor and fight a battle as if I were fighting a physical fight. People may not have understood what I was going through, but I knew that this thing would continue to affect other generations if I didn't fight. I had to learn how to pray to defend my children. So, I prayed for God's strength to help me so that I can finally finish this battle once and for all and ensure that my children, grandchildren, great-grandchildren, and the unborn generation will not have to endure this faulty foundation.

As I mentioned earlier, pregnant women should be cautious with sacrifices. Once you conceive, there is no room for excuses; you need to start the midnight battle and cover those children. Most times, they use unborn children to nurture their altars, which This is why you see even governments legalising abortion, because the baby is sinless, and that is the highest sacrifice to the satanic Kingdom.

This is even worse when you have someone close to you, maybe a father, a mother, an uncle, a brother, or a sister—who is still practicing devil worship. It won't be easy because you have an immediate family member who submits themselves there. However, if you have begun the deliverance journey, God, in His mercy, will reveal everything that is happening, and the deliverance minister will provide guidance on what to do next, all with the Lord's help.

When I was growing up, we used to bury at least one person or two a year. Perhaps from the 1980s until 2014, it was the case that someone had to die each year via abortion, accident, sudden death, or sickness. I asked God why this was so, and my eyes were opened to see that there was somebody who was a demonic priest causing these deaths of people in my family/clan. There were still some satanic portals and covenants in place that our forefathers left, and no one had an idea how to shut them and open the Godly portal. As the Bible says, *our fathers have eaten sour grapes, and the children's teeth are set on edge.*

PORTALS:

What is the Portal?

Spiritual portals and Godly portals are often understood as divine access points or gateways through which God's presence, power, and revelation are made manifest in the natural realm. In biblical and spiritual contexts, a portal is not a literal door but a symbolic or supernatural opening that allows heavenly realities to intersect with earthly experiences. These portals can be opened through acts of worship, prayer, fasting, obedience, and divine encounters. For instance, in the Bible, locations such as Bethel (where Jacob saw the ladder reaching to heaven) or the temple in Jerusalem are considered places where heaven touched earth spiritual portals where God's presence was especially tangible.

Godly portals are believed to be aligned with the will and purpose of God, offering believers unique moments of divine visitation, spiritual breakthrough, or prophetic revelation. They can occur in specific places, seasons, or during sacred activities where God chooses to reveal Himself more deeply. These moments or "portals" are often marked by a heightened sense of God's glory, clarity of spiritual vision, and a call to deeper intimacy with Him. Unlike occult or ungodly spiritual gateways that seek power apart from God, Godly portals are rooted in the authority and holiness of God and lead to transformation, alignment with

His will, and empowerment for service. In essence, spiritual and Godly portals remind us that the spiritual and physical realms are deeply connected, and that God sovereignly chooses moments and means by which He draws near to His people.

Closing Satanic Portals and Opening Godly Ones

All believers, as serious children of God, need to walk in complete deliverance, we must become experts in spiritual portals. Closing portals of hell and opening portals of heaven.

Satanic portals are often opened through sin, wicked altars, generational covenants, and dark rituals. These portals allow demonic access to lives, families, cities, and even nations. But when a believer becomes serious with God, Satan recognizes the threat and dispatches his greatest weapons from the five kingdoms to stop them. He doesn't waste his resources on those who aren't a threat, but the moment you seek true deliverance and alignment with God, all hell breaks loose to oppose you.

Sometimes, the person consistently attacking or resisting you may be a representative of a portal of hell. You cannot overcome them until that portal is closed and a portal of heaven is opened right where you are, even in your office. Your office should become more than just a workspace; it should become a portal of heaven, where angels ascend and descend. Your chair, your desk, everything can be a gate to the divine presence.

Where satanic portals exist, demons and spirits from hell infiltrate and influence entire organizations. That's why we must be intentional: close every demonic portal and open godly ones. Learn to specialize in opening portals of heaven in cities, territories, and nations to bring revival. Travel through nations, shutting portals of hell and opening portals of healing, deliverance, and restoration. You are becoming a spiritual expert in portals.

Some of us are literally sleeping on portals of hell. The location of your house, your bed, or even your room might have been a portal opened through acts of sin, perhaps someone previously engaged in fornication there. Go back and shut that portal. Open a godly one through repentance, worship, and the blood of Jesus.

You may have a great idea, business, career, or ministry, but if a satanic portal is controlling your life, everything will be tied to darkness. Some are sick because of a portal of sickness in your home. Others are trapped in poverty due to a wasting portal, a place where demonic activity drains resources. When you close that portal, the witches will leave, because demons, spirits, cannot stay where there is no portal open to them.

In both villages and cities, portals empower the work of witchcraft. Occultists prosper because they know where these portals are. They go there at night barefoot to reopen them and capture souls. They walk across the city, maintaining access points for demonic activity. Until the Church rises and locates these portals to shut them down and open heavenly portals, we will not see true revival.

False prophets operate through demonic portals. Some synagogues and churches are built on portals of hell. People go to worship and are unknowingly captured by the spirits operating through those gates. Many of you lost your money, your star, your destiny at such portals, but the time has come to close them and recover what was lost in the name of Jesus.

Deep Spiritual Battles Require Portal Awareness

You cannot win deep spiritual battles without closing the portals of hell. Areas where prostitutes gather, bars, and nightclubs are not just physical places; they are spiritual gateways that must be shut. If not, your children may one day pass through them and fall under the same bondage.

Many satanic hotels are built on portals of hell. Jesus Himself travelled across the sea for one purpose: to close a portal. He stood on a rock and declared, "On this rock I will build My Church, and the gates of hell shall not prevail against it." That rock was a known gate of hell, but Jesus announced a new beginning, a portal of heaven and authority for His people.

In every city, there are portals of hell on hills, near seaports, even in areas where false prophets, pastors, and witches gather. Some church leaders are aware of the portals under their pulpits, active portals of darkness, yet they take no action.

Jesus told Nathanael, "You will see heaven open, and angels ascending and descending upon the Son of Man." He was describing a portal. John 1:51. When Jacob woke from his dream, he said, "Surely the Lord is in this place, this is none other than the house of God, the gate of heaven. Genesis 28:16" That place was a portal of God that's why heavenly angels had access to it, ascending and descending.

A portal can be fixed to a specific location or attached to a mobile device. When Israel travelled through the wilderness, a cloud followed them, a divine portal in motion. Wherever they went, the presence of God was with them. Exodus 40:36-38 Throughout all the travels of the Israelites, whenever the cloud lifted from above the tabernacle, they set out; but if the cloud did not lift, they did not set out—until the day it lifted. So, the cloud of the Lord was over the tabernacle by day, and fire was in the cloud by night, in the sight of all the Israelites during all their journeys.

I declare that everywhere you go, there will be an open heaven over your life. Imagine if both a portal is open on you and another in the place where you are when heaven is upon your life and the location is consecrated to God's presence.

I pray that many of us will be serious about opening heavenly portals that subdue portals of hell, and usher in the move of God that will build a larger portal of prayer by shutting the gates of hell and stirring end-time church revival.

When the portal of heaven is open, healing, deliverance, and miracles flow. When Peter walked, a portal moved with him, his shadow healed the sick because heaven rested on him. He didn't need to struggle in prayer; people were healed simply by coming into the portal's reach. Acts 5:15 As a result, people brought the sick into the streets and laid them on beds and mats so that at least Peter's shadow might fall on some of them as he passed by.

The Spirit of the Lord told me that I could stop the foundational evil simply by speaking and reversing the evil through closing the evil portal and opening the Godly portal into the foundation. I decided to speak the word and began to observe things manifesting immediately, I noticed premature deaths were cut off and all other negative cycles and patterns. If I had known this before, I would have stopped so many deaths in my foundation. I remember I said in 2014, on my brother's grave, that this would be the last satanic/untimely death of anybody in my bloodline. Whoever decides to follow the God I follow, Jesus Christ of Nazareth, will never face premature death, for the Lord God Almighty will reveal it to me before it comes, and it will be reversed. I thank God that He has been revealing many things, and many lives have been saved from death. Since then, there have been no unexpected premature deaths in my family tree. Even my family members can attest to that. Our God is merciful, faithful, and wonderful. Our God is good.

So, the part of the strong man and the stronghold is for them to steal, kill, and destroy silently; they are working so hard to complete the assignment in their covenants without wasting time. Watch and pray, decree things, command things; the word of God is in control, and so, you are in control, you are prevailing in the name of Jesus.

Chapter 4:
Altars

The contention that you see is because there is an active altar speaking. The altar that your forefathers built is the one that is fighting you. Now, as a child of God, you need to raise an altar that represents the kingdom of our Lord Jesus Christ. It's imperative to build an altar because the altar that is speaking is one from a faulty foundation, and that is why it's battling you and resisting everything you try to do in Christ Jesus. So, you will need to take the altar down and raise another one; it's an altar versus altar situation.

Your altar will be mighty because God is the greatest altar, and that will overpower every other. When you build an altar to Jesus Christ, you literally open the portal to the realm of His glory. Angels are ascending and descending for spiritual activities. When you plant that altar, divine intervention comes into place to establish the Kingdom. Angels will ascend and descend frequently because they can locate the portal you have opened for God. When you build an altar, you are saying, *'Jesus, come down on my altar and establish Your Kingdom in my family, my nation, my generation, my bloodline, or my lineage.'*

That is what it means when you build an altar. An altar is different from a prayer meeting. We pray, we fast, and sometimes we intensify our devotion by erecting an altar. Now, when you build an altar, it demonstrates your seriousness because you must establish something in Christ Jesus that supersedes what was done before in your life or family.

Just like Jesus said, this kind cannot come out except by prayer and fasting. It demonstrates the seriousness with which you must approach your spiritual practice: you have an altar in place when you pray and fast. This is another level in the journey of deliverance. You must establish a foundation upon which to stand when you begin calling on Jesus.

Of course, the ultimate altar is the Altar of the Cross of Jesus. In the book of Exodus 20:24, God commanded Moses to make an altar on earth for Him, to sacrifice a burnt offering, and to make a fellowship offering of sheep, goats, and cattle. Then He said, *If you make that altar for me, I will do three things for you*:

1. *I will cause my name to be honored.* Another version says *I will record my name on what you're going to pray for on this altar*. When you have an altar, that means God is recording His name right there.

2. *My presence will be there.* The presence of God is with us because we pray together with Christ. The altar is to Jesus Christ; the presence of Jesus Christ is present.

3. *I will bless you.* In other words, you will not be the same again. The blessings of grace are the blessings of Abraham, Isaac, and Jacob.

Those are the beautiful things that happen when you build an altar. I pray that God will give you the grace to see the benefit of the altar deeply and raise one so that you don't miss out.

In the Book of Matthew 18:18, Jesus Christ says, '*I tell you the truth: whatever you bind on earth is bound in heaven; whatever you loose on earth is loosed in heaven.*'

In verse 20, it is written, **"For where two or three are gathered together in my name, there I am in the midst of them."** When we build an altar in His name, He shows up;

Yes, God is omnipresent but the altar draws His attention to you in a special way. Additionally, when we do so, we come together in unity, as the Father, the Son, and the Holy Spirit.

And when we build an altar, He gives us authority. After you come in the name of Jesus Christ of Nazareth, you receive the power the power of God to work within you. The power of God begins to function. Job 22:28 says, *You will decree a thing, and it shall come to pass.* So, when you declare and take authority, just believe it is established.

The kingdom of darkness takes their altars and sacrifices very seriously because that is their portal. I had to take the issue of altars very seriously after I realized that my enemies were operating from the altar. Before that, I did not feel the importance of it. Until I raised one in the name of Jesus Christ, that's when I began to see many changes, even in the foundational battles. I'm trying to protect my deliverance because I have done extensive work in this area so far, and I must safeguard what I have accomplished over the years. I've done extensive work over the years, and I won't allow that progress to be undone. I refuse to bring it this far only to abandon it now.

Ensure that the altar that was present in the foundation is demolished as you construct your altar in the name of Jesus. Gideon received instructions to destroy the altar.

There is power in a spiritual altar; it attracts powers, depending on the god to which it is dedicated. Is it dedicated to water spirits, mermaids, serpentine, marine spirits, spouses, strange meetings in dreams, or witchcraft? All this can be revealed in your dream. It is very important that you examine the altar you serve or the altar your foundation or family serves.

Make sure to tear down all the demonic altars in your foundation, your bloodline- your mother's side and your father's side. Unfortunately, the children of God have been so ignorant of the things of the spirit; we tend to ignore them, yet they are the ones affecting us so much. But this is the correct route to take. There is no easy option; if you want your foundation cleaned, there is no alternative.

The Bible says, "*The fear of the Lord is the beginning of wisdom.* One thing I can assure you is that if someone has gone through this kind of deliverance, they don't take the things of God lightly. They fear the Lord. They are down and trembling because it's been such an arduous and painful journey. These kinds of people lead people toward the right way —to Christ —and tell them the truth that deliverance is possible, guiding them into repentance.

What Do You Need to Tear Down the Altar

Faith is the first thing you need to tear down the altar; faith is the engine of deliverance. Faith in the Word of God generates the power of God. When you have faith on board, you possess the power of God, the strength of God, and the authority of God. In the book of Matthew 21:21, He said. *If you believe, you will receive whatever you ask.* When you have faith in Jesus Christ, He will give you power. You will do His work. The Word of the Lord to Zerubbabel was: *'I want you to do something, but it's not by might, nor by power, but by the Spirit of the living, all-mighty God.'* Faith in God releases His power to tear down every opposing altar.

Now, the second thing you need when tearing down the altar is a declaration. *I declare in the name of Jesus Christ of Nazareth that this demonic altar is uprooted. We declare that it will be neutralized. We pull down the strongholds over this household*. It's very important to tear down those altars and then begin to build good ones.

> *Job 22:28: You will decree a thing, and it will be established to you.*

So, we tear down evil altars by declaring. And then, the third thing to do as you tear down the evil altar is to replace it by building a godly altar, thereby replacing the one you have torn down.

> *Jeremiah 1:10: See, today I appoint you of a nation to uproot, tear down, destroy, overthrow, build, and plant.*

Whatever demonic altar in this family that was raised due to greed, selfishness, ignorance, and poverty, I tear it down. I neutralize it by the blood of Jesus Christ in the mighty name of Jesus Christ of Nazareth, in accordance with the Word of God with faith. You need to speak to Satan in the name of Jesus. You no longer have power in this family. You no longer have power in this foundation. You no longer have influence in this place. Because I am going to build an altar in the name of Jesus Christ of Nazareth. Therefore, in the name of Jesus, I tear you down; I destroy you down in the name of Jesus, I overthrow you, according to Jeremiah in the name of Jesus. Your head is broken, and your arm is broken. You no longer have influence, and you no longer have authority in this place. In the name of Jesus Christ, you no longer have authority in this bloodline, In this generation, in this foundation. By the blood of Jesus Christ of Nazareth, the name of Jesus Christ prevails, and the word of Jesus Christ prevails. What I bind on earth is bound in heaven; what I lose on earth is loosed in heaven, and I lose in the name of Jesus all strongholds in this place. I cut you off. I cut your chains; I burn you up with a consuming fire.

Hebrews 12:29: My God is a consuming fire.

Pray;

Every evil plantation in my foundation and in my bloodline that God did not plant, I command consuming fire to consume it, and it will not be there again. Now, I build a divine and proper altar to Jesus Christ. And I raise an adequate altar to Jesus Christ of Nazareth.

Chapter 5:
Family Members Under Devil Worshiping

Family members who are still connected to the Kingdom of Darkness- how does this affect someone who is seeking foundational deliverance? In the book of Leviticus 18:21, the Bible says,

> *Do not give any of your children to be sacrificed to Moleki, for you must not bring shame on the name of the Lord. I am your God,*

This means every time someone submits under this Kingdom, it brings shame to the name of our God and also to the Kingdom of God. So, as a child of God, you are engaged in deliverance; you are working diligently to do everything possible and right before the Lord. But just next to you, there is another person who is working tirelessly against you through the other kingdom of darkness to hinder the mission of God in your life and thwart your God-given destiny. That's why you find that deliverance for such persons is very complicated; he has to come to understand the people surrounding him immediate family members and friends because once you begin the journey of deliverance, God, in His mercy, works and walks with you every step of the way. The Spirit of the Lord enters you as a vessel and begins to lead and guide. He's with you through the fire, storm, through the valley, and the mountain. He is with you, and he not only works with you but also walks with you; He equips you. Then you'll have to take on this journey of deliverance very seriously. Since you are equipped, your prayers become the greatest weapon of warfare; every prayer you release shifts things in the kingdom of darkness.

It is a prayer that is loaded with the weapons of war, which is the Power of God. Everything you release with understanding and authority goes straight to the kingdom of darkness. You begin to see that the Lord is working side by side with you. He begins to show you, through dreams or visions, what exactly you need to tackle and what is going on. God shows you a glimpse, like a movie, of what your warfare prayers are doing in the Kingdom of darkness. That's how you receive the strength to keep going in your fight, because you can see how you are advancing in the Spiritual Realm.

Things that will keep you growing strong, remaining standing, and advancing in the spiritual realm or the supernatural realm are midnight battles, fasting, consecration, discipline and consistency in prayer. This is how you can take down your enemies. But the enemy is not just watching; he is also fighting. The enemies are increasing their power, enhancing their weapons, and seeking to counter the effect of your warfare.

That's what you see on the spiritual battlefield: we increase in authority and command according to how the voice of God leads us in warfare, and our arrows hit the target. When the arrows are too many, the fire is too great. This affects them, and the entire kingdom begins to shake and fall apart; now they understand that they are not dealing with just a human being, but with an anointing and an authority. So, what do they do? They increase pressure. Remember, I told you they cannot easily give up because they have so much invested in you through your name, your stars, your generation, and your foundation.

So, they're not going to give up easily; a battle is expected and not to be underestimated. Giving up means surrendering everything they have stolen from your foundation, that they have taken from your ignorant people. So, if they don't increase the warfare against you, they must give up what is making them well-off, famous, and prosperous here on earth. That's why they will intensify the fight and contend with you. Remember everything that Satan has either stolen from you or put on you. The battle aims to let go of what Satan has stolen and exchanged from you and your people.

They will increase the warfare and pressure on the person connected to you who submits to their kingdom. They will torment them so they can come after you. To them, it's all about their kingdom, nothing less. They don't care about the lives lost or the pain they are causing; they don't care. So, these are the satanic agents connected to you. They must do what they are asked to do, regardless of their affection towards you. This is the point when they can even take your life down and kill you because you are disturbing them and blocking their evil agendas. This is very important for the children of God when you begin to demand what is rightfully yours. Remember, He is watching very closely; the Bible says, '*He who sits in Heaven shall laugh.*' There is automatic heavenly diplomatic Immunity to you. There is nothing Satan can do to you; you are highly protected, seated at the right hand of the father with Christ Jesus. God cannot put you in the forefront and abandon you; it is impossible. He is the one doing the work; you are just a vessel He chose to use to bring deliverance to your foundation and to His people. I pray that you will be the one to bring foundational victory to your family.

That is why once they label you as a threat, you become their target, and their wish is for your downfall so that you will fight and pray no more against them. The anointing on you is to pursue, overtake, and recover all without fail. To continually maintain your position in the battle, you must keep your fire burning; you must maintain purity, holiness, and righteousness, and the fear of the Lord should not depart from you. That's why some of us have reached the point of not going back, and we wage war like mad prophets. It is a daily battle at our Altar of Deliverance, known as Jesus Deliverance Clinic International Ministries, and it is our daily midnight platform that the enemy fears so much due to the consistency and discipline we have maintained over the past few years. Every midnight, we wage war. These are the reasons for the fire burning continually.

God said at the beginning of this year that He is looking for people who are consistent. When you are consistent, you'll surely be able to overcome this dark kingdom with the help of the Lord Jesus Christ. The enemy conducts research on us and calculates how far we can fight; the enemy understands us much better than we know ourselves. There is no way you can fail to take them down when you are consistent. Every time you are on the altar, you are strengthening your spiritual muscles and moving deeper into realms through prayer and the Word of God.

If you are consistent in doing this every day, you will inevitably change. Every day, you attain new realms of power and prayer and authority. However, when you are partial, you'll miss out on what a full-time warrior can achieve, both in spirit and physical realms. In our ministry, we are only full-time and overtime because the battles we are fighting are not the battles of the part-time people. We are advancing in the spirit realm daily, capturing territories and nations, for that is what we are called to do as the *Nehemiah' Generation*, to build the broken walls and restore. We are the *John the Baptist Generation*, to take it from the enemy by fire and force; the Jehu generation, to demolish kings and their evil seed.

CURSE:

A curse is a declaration, often spoken or written, that brings harm, misfortune, or negative consequences upon a person, place, or group. In spiritual and biblical terms, it is often seen as a judgment or consequence resulting from disobedience to God, such as sin or breaking divine covenants. Curses can affect individuals, families, or even nations, sometimes extending across generations. In Scripture, curses are the opposite of blessings—while blessings bring favor and protection, curses bring suffering and hardship. Deuteronomy 28 clearly outlines this contrast, linking obedience to blessings and disobedience to curses. In many cultures, curses are also believed to result from spells or rituals. However, in Christianity, the death and resurrection of Jesus Christ provide the power to break every curse, especially those rooted in sin or spiritual oppression. Through faith, confession, renunciation, repentance, and cleansing prayer, believers can be freed from curses and restored to a life of blessing.

> *Proverbs 26:2: Like a spiral in its fleeting, like a swallow in its flying. So, a curse without a course shall not stand.*

So many religious people- born again, children of God- take this verse lackadaisically. When we utter a curse without a valid reason, such as a fleeting spiral or a swiftly flying swallow, it will have no impact and won't "*land*" on its intended target. Yes, I agree, but what you are forgetting is that Leviticus 18:21 says, *Do not give any of your children to be sacrificed. Moleki, but it must not bring shame to the name of God.*

Some people in your bloodline and foundation are still giving their children to the kingdom of darkness for sacrifice. This means that, since they are connected to you via the bloodline, it could work against you. They are furious yet content and determined that you will never stand on your ground with God. This is the time when you need to be strategic in your warfare and ensure your aircraft flies above all the mountains and turbulence, so you don't crash, allowing you to remain above the enemy and keep the fire prayer burning. Otherwise, you will end up giving up, feeling disappointed, and ultimately failing in your mission. The Bible says.

Psalms 110:1: The Lord says to my lord: "Sit at my right hand until I make your enemies a footstool for your feet.

And that's how all your enemies become casualties and die because they are under your feet.

The Kingdom of Darkness is quite content with its current state. They are full-time employees— they are disciplined in their work. They are not part-time like many of us children of God. They work tirelessly to ensure that you are not undermining their kingdom. They influence individuals in families to oppress others; that's when you hear someone say, *'I was bewitching my child, but it was not my will.'* *'I was submitting my brothers, my sister, and young children to the demonic kingdom, but it was not my will.'* They will target the weakest link in your life to do exactly what they want because they know that person is the best candidate to reveal secrets about the person of interest in the family who is an active threat to their kingdom.

If you can sustain this battle, you will not only win for yourself, but you will also win for your entire generation. The Bible says.

Proverb 6:31: Yet if he is caught, he must pay sevenfold, though it costs him all the wealth of his house.

When God delivers, He delivers ultimately. All that the locusts have eaten, God brings together the palmerworm, the caterpillar, and restores at the same time. That is what they are fighting against; they don't want to lose their hold over the past generations (and sometimes even over the unborn generation). That's why you need to stand and fight. It is genuinely chaotic in their demonic camp, and they are surprised because no one has ever gone this far to acquire such knowledge and begin to shake them.

The Bible says some arrows fly by day, and some arrows fly by night. So, if they can't catch you at night because you are busy praying, they will prey on you during the day, when you are careless. Why do they have to send the arrows at night if they can get you in the day? They will get you at your careless moment. This is to enlighten those who are serious about deliverance: You must always ensure that you are immersed in the blood of Jesus, and you can intercede behind the scenes. Be aware that your enemies are working diligently to ensure they bring you down, alive or dead.

This is the time when you must ensure that the whole armor of God is on you, not just you, but also your children, your wife, your husband, your brothers, and your sisters. Because if they can't get you, they must make sure they get anyone close to you. So, this is the time. You don't have to go looking for one righteous person to break the chains; you have become the righteous person. The full manifestation of your destiny is glorious and shining— it's a burning and shining light, the blessing of Abraham, Isaac, and Jacob, full of the glory of God. Your destiny is loaded with everything.

My assignment is to ensure that people understand these things and diligently work on their destiny so that they will not miss out on the beautiful purpose for which the Lord has created them. Additionally, if you are not fully embracing your destiny, God cannot use you fully as He intends. For these reasons, you will be incubated until you are enlightened in this way and begin to work toward fulfilling your purpose. Then, God will be able to release exactly what you need. Also, in the book of Galatians 3:13, the Bible says

Christ redeemed us from the curse of the law, having become a curse for us, for it is written, 'Cursed is everyone who hangs on a tree. '

Yes, He redeemed us from the curse of the law. When you read a verse like this, you tend to encourage yourself that there is no need to do anything, for Jesus has finished it all. Yes, Jesus did, but this doesn't mean that you can live in sin because Jesus finished it all. This does not mean that you cannot confess, renounce, or repent because Jesus has finished it all. We are still required to live a very careful and disciplined holy life.

Leviticus 18:21: Do not give any of your children to be a sacrifice to monitor, for you must not bring shame on the name of the Lord. I am your God

As long as you still have people connected to you who submit to the kingdom of darkness, the curse will still be in place in your family/generation. Of course, as a born-again Christian, if you die today, you will go to heaven, but your life and that of your loved ones will remain bound until someone raises the trumpet to rescue them.

This is why God is trusting you. That's why God says, *I am looking for one righteous person, for the secret of the Kingdom is for the righteous.* He knows what a righteous person can do and how far can go. To reach a state of righteousness, you must have worked diligently and understood the high price of holiness and what it can achieve. God honors the righteous; He loads you with His glory, and you can tear down the kingdom of darkness under His authority. In this way, you'll be able to expose the people connected to you who are submitting to the kingdom of darkness. God works with you side by side because He can trust you.

You are not a person who always gives excuses; you are not someone who finds reasons not to do the work of God. And when God is on your side, you know victory is guaranteed. You refuse to give up; you refuse to leave any of your goods in the hands of Satan. As you fight to deliver yourself, you are being used as a vessel of deliverance for your family. Then God places a mantle on you to begin delivering territories and nations. He amplifies your voice, and the powers of darkness flee when they hear you are in their territory. You tear down the Kingdom of Darkness, and eventually, anyone connected to you, any shrine, or any demonic altar built begins to crumble and fall. The continuous sacrifices that have been made begin to be nullified by the power of God.

The Bible says in John that *You are a burning and a shining light.*

So, you are bringing light to darkness. And everyone else eventually will come to light and submit to your God. We pray for God to bring salvation to our people and our immediate family members. When prayer is consistent and done with profound understanding, the kingdom of darkness will begin to retreat.

And they have no choice except to submit to the lordship of Jesus. These days, we see people from the dark kingdom abandoning their assignments because when we say, *'Fire on your shrine, fire,'* the fire falls on their shrines, and they begin to run in the spiritual realm. A prayer of authority can accomplish much and can even shut down the work of the entire kingdom. We all need to reach this point of authority when we represent Jesus; the same power that raised Him from the dead is within us if we consecrate our bodies as the temples of the Lord Jesus Christ.

There is a prayer point that we pray often: *Let all their transportation systems crash land to irretrievable pieces.* Indeed, they will fall and bash land to pieces in the mighty name of Jesus Christ. Another prayer point: *I disrupt all their communication systems. I shut down first and second heaven by the power that raised Jesus from the dead, which means they can't communicate.* There is no communication between the agents on earth and the higher powers of darkness, including principality, power, might, and dominion, in the 1st and 2nd heavens.

> **Ephesians 1:20-22: "Which He worked in Christ when He raised Him from the dead and seated Him at His right hand in the heavenly places, far above all principality and power and might and dominion, and every name that is named, not only in this age but also in the one to come."**

Your prayer is disrupting their communication system, meaning you have thwarted all their plans for that day. However, they don't tire easily; tomorrow, they will try again. This is when you say, "By the power in the mighty name of Jesus Christ, I scatter their satellites and mirrors." What are they doing with their mirrors? They are monitoring every step of your destiny, tracking your daily schedule. In essence, they have control over your life. This is why they plan death, accidents, sacrifice, confusion, contention, disappointment, failure, disgrace, fear and more. They have special agents called monitoring spirits (This could be physical or spiritual)" who are observing you spiritually from a satanic satellite and mirror monitoring your present and future and they hold a remote control over your life.

When you scatter their satellites, mirrors, and transportation systems, they can no longer access your life. The next time they try to call you in their mirror; the face of

Jesus Christ will appear. We always pray this prayer: "This time, when they call my name, when they mention my family name, or when they mention my family members or children, let fire answer!" And indeed, the fire will answer. When you begin to engage in such warfare, you will see that they can no longer claim dominion over you. They will confess they can't afford you anymore, and they will flee from you.

This is when you experience a release. You will begin to see the kingdoms of darkness fall, one after another. If you find yourself battling specific forces in your dreams, like snakes, you will start to kill them. If they serve the god of water, those affected may experience issues such as spiritual marriages. In such cases, you will begin to decapitate the spirit spouses in your dreams whether they appear as your husband, wife, or even someone from your past with whom you still carry an unresolved soul tie.

When you see these spirits, take up the double-edged sword and begin to decapitate them, even in the dream. God will grant you the grace to see them in your dreams, deal with them, and finish the battle there. This is how we tear down kingdom after kingdom. If you see a mermaid in your dream, this signifies the marine kingdom at work in your life. You may feel anger or desperation in the dream, but this is because your inner self is awake and alert, even while you are sleeping. Release fire upon the mermaid, for she is there to steal, kill, and destroy. As you pray, you will see the mermaids falling and catching fire. You will begin to win the war in the dream itself.

This is deliverance, and being serious about deliverance means entering the secret place as a child of God who is both angry and desperate in the spirit. You are not here just for yourself but for the bloodline. You declare, "*Let my people go,"* as Moses did. It's time for the people of God to worship the Lord, and you, child of God, are the vessel through which that can happen.

The Bible says in Jeremiah 33:3, *"Call unto me, and I will answer and show you unsearchable things you do not know."* I like to pair this with James 4:7: *"Submit to God. Resist the devil, and he will flee from you."* First, you must submit. How do you submit? By staying in the secret place, cultivating intimacy with God. Be His friend, and let His Word touch your heart, not just your mouth.

> **Proverbs 4:23:** *"Above all else, guard your heart, for everything you do flows from it."*

Why is this important? Many Christians today focus on salvation as something spoken with the mouth, but God pays more attention to the condition of our hearts, thoughts, and actions when no one is watching. We must seek to know God deeply seeking that father-son intimacy. This is called a sonship relationship. As you grow closer to the Lord, He will reveal crucial things to you for your deliverance.

This is why staying close to God is important. If God is not in the fight, you will be battling on your own, and I can assure you that you will lose. In deliverance, we don't aim to lose because the consequences of losing are not pleasant. Even in daily prayers, God will show you exactly what to pray for. He will reveal both the good and the bad people in your life and how to deal with them without causing unnecessary conflict.

When God began showing me, I was shocked that people I trusted and considered close friends began appearing in my dreams. I saw them bewitching, not just once, but many times. I saw family members with ill intentions toward me. God shows us these things so we can be cautious. What we see in the spirit realm often differs from what we experience in the physical world. The Bible says, *"Call me, and I will show you unsearchable things."* Many people look for witches far away, but the true witch may be someone close to you someone you would never suspect.

The enemy's first strategy is to use a demonic agent close to you because they know you well and can operate without raising suspicion. You trust them, share meals, clothes, and your life with them, but they are on an assignment, whether male or female. This is why the Bible says, *"Call unto me, and I will show you unsearchable things your mind cannot fathom."* You might discover that a mother is controlling her daughter through witchcraft, causing repeated miscarriages for sacrifice. The truth is, it's not the mother herself but a spirit controlling her. These are unsearchable things, difficult to believe, but true.

When I tell you to submit entirely to God, He will enlighten you. He will reveal things to you; you won't need to get angry. It will be beautiful because you will know how to fight effectively. The Bible says in Ephesians 6:12, *"For we do not wrestle against flesh and blood, but against principalities, against powers, against the rulers of the darkness of this age, against spiritual hosts of wickedness in heavenly places."*

In deliverance, you don't focus on a person when you see evil manifesting in the dream. Whether it's a friend, brother, cousin, or family member, focus on the spirit behind it. The real enemy is the power at work within them. Address the spirit directly at your altar, and fire your prayers accordingly.

Chapter 6:
Fear as A Satanic Weapon

Fear is a natural emotional response to perceived danger or threat, helping us stay safe by activating the body's "fight or flight" reaction. It can be triggered by real situations or imagined fears such as failure of the unknown. While fear can protect us, it becomes harmful when it is constant or irrational, leading to anxiety, stress, and health issues. Spiritually, fear is viewed in two ways: the fear of God, which means reverence and awe, and fear of the world, which involves worry and insecurity. The Bible encourages believers not to live in fear, reminding them through verses like Isaiah 41:10 that God's presence brings peace and courage. Through faith and trust in God, fear can be replaced with confidence and inner peace. Fear is the most effective weapon that Satan uses on people going through deliverance. Whenever someone engages in warfare against the satanic kingdom, their efforts are often met with resistance when the enemy disrupts their work and launches counter attacks.

One such attack is fear. Why is the enemy inflicting fear? Remember that if you are the first to seek deliverance in your family, your foundation has never been affected by such warfare prayers. The enemy has been so comfortable in your foundation and has no plans to leave. The foundation has been under satanic watch and satanic manipulation for ages, from generation to generation.

In His mercy, the Lord will place a special anointing on one person to seek the deliverance of the entire bloodline. God is touching your heart and calling you to be the one He has chosen to deliver your generation. In other words, you are the one to put a stop to the oppression, to stand and tell

Satan, *Here I come, not in my name, but in the name of Jesus. The reason I am coming now is that amazing grace has found me. I was blind, but now I see. What I see is a faulty foundation, a generation that worships the devil, a disobedient generation and a rebellious generation. A generation that has no fear of God. What I see is a foundation that carries guilt. What I see is a foundation that needs God's mercy. That being said, I will not sit quietly and watch. I will put on the mantle of Jehu and rise to demolish the house of any Ahab and Jezebel that is still around my foundation, causing it to sink deeper and deeper into satanism. I will rise as Esther to rescue a nation, my people, my bloodline. I will increase as Moses to deliver my family, the captives. I will rise like Deborah to erase an old law that was written by evil men in my foundation and write a new law that favors the children of God in my foundation and a law that introduces Christ and brings light.*

Mathew 16:18: And I tell you that you are Peter, and on this rock, I will build my church, and the gates of Hades will not overcome it.

So, when you speak, you announce it to the enemy. The Bible says, *You shall know the truth; it shall set you free.*

The enemy likes people who are Christians but ignorant; he has no problem with them. They can quote Bible verses from Genesis to Revelation, but they are still powerless. The enemy is not afraid of them because he, too, knows the scriptures. The enemy fears Christians who possess the fire of God, the power of God, boldness, a deep understanding of their identity in Christ, and a zeal for God, the authority they have in Christ Jesus. The moment you open yourself up to the knowledge of God, the Holy Spirit is faithful to impart to you with seven spirits of the Lord, which are knowledge, understanding, wisdom, spirit of God, spirit of the fear of the

Lord, spirit of Might, spirit of counsel. You will be empowered to the point where you can barely comprehend. You will find yourself entering another realm of the Spirit because God is looking for people like that. People make a mockery of the children of God because they have been casualties of the enemy the enemy is laughing at them and asking, *Where is your God now?*

> **Psalms 42:10: My bones suffer mortal agony as my foes taunt me, saying to me all day long, "Where is your God?"**

There's a need for people of *God to rise and say God is not in this situation; it is the work of Satan, and Jesus came to destroy the works of the enemy. This negativity- pain, disease, poverty, struggles, hard life, afflictions, addictions, and premature death— is not what the Bible says; it's not what God said. So, if there is any satanic manipulation, I must dig deeper.* Note that when you start digging deep, you prompt God to reveal mysteries to you, for *if there is a man to dig deeper, there is a God to reveal the hidden secrets.*

> **Daniel 2:22: He reveals the deep and secret things.**

When you go deep, the Lord also reveals the more profound things; secrets are hidden in the depths. Even Peter had to cast his net into the deep.

> **Psalms 42:7: Deep calls to deep in the roar of your waterfalls; all your waves and breakers have swept over me.**

Many Christians are still in the shallows. Do you see how God works? God will release things to you according to the level of your faith and your strength in Him. If you decide to stay shallow, He will also give you *shallow* until you can stretch yourself a little more. But when you read Bible verses like this, you know that there are more profound things, and that will help you press in so that He can reveal more to you. If something is profound, you need to be even more profound to address it effectively. If something is profound, you can't remain superficial and expect to solve the deeper issues; you must delve into the spiritual realm. In this realm, you meet God in the secret place. That's where God is going to begin the discussion with you, as it says in the Book of Isaiah 41:21, *Present your case, says the Lord; send forth your argument; let us argue together.*

Now you sit with God- Abba, the King of Kings, the King of Glory, the God of all gods, the God of all flesh. Here, you surrender to Him because you recognize that this is beyond your control; you have done what you can fasted and prayed but you are unable to turn the negative situation. The more you do this, the more the battle increases. So, you ask Him to reveal every secret or hidden agenda.

> **Isaiah 43:26: *Review the past for me, let us argue the matter together; state the case for your innocence.***

You must understand that when the enemy has been undermining your foundation for a long time, what they have done has stripped away your authority. So, even though you are waging war, your dominion has been usurped.

> **Daniel 7:12: *The other beasts had been stripped of their authority but were allowed to live for a period of time***

Authority can be stripped off. Why is the enemy succeeding? Because the enemy has authority over you, controlling you remotely. You are working, but you have lost your dominion to Satan. That's why the Bible says in Genesis 1:28,

God blessed them and said to them, "Be fruitful and multiply; fill the earth and subdue it. Rule over the fish in the sea, the birds in the sky, and over every living creature that moves on the ground.

But you cannot win the battle if you have no dominion; you have no authority. That is why it is very important to inquire of the Lord. And the Lord will reveal to you precisely what is happening as you wage war to reclaim your dominion, authority, and throne, so you can begin to fight, command, and declare from a position of authority. In the book of Hosea 14:2 "Take words with you and return to the Lord. Say to him: 'Forgive all our sins and receive us graciously, that we may offer the fruit of our lips.'"

This is the moment when you realize you've had enough. You have already understood that there's a problem, and they are already aware that their hold on your family is coming to an end.

At this point, many will give up and decide to have nothing to do with deliverance, settling for less and saying, *'Let me continue with what I have.'* But few choose to pursue, overtake, and recover all. Those are the people that God is looking for, and He equips them.

I struggled at the beginning of the deliverance process; it felt like a struggle. The enemy oppresses you to the point that you ask God if He's there. But the Lord God is with you in His might. That's why you have the strength to wake up the next day and forge ahead. However, the enemy usually pushes back: you may experience sudden losses, attacks that feel like severe migraine headaches, disappointment, and confusion in families. All these are designed to distract you from focusing on what you are doing, from unseating the enemy from your throne, and reclaiming your throne. At this point, you need to be content, no matter what the enemy throws at you, because you know you are engaged in a process of deliverance, and you must be delivered. Dress up with the whole armor of God, and continue, for the Lord is with you.

Before embarking on deliverance, you need to prepare: you have to fast and consecrate yourself. Ensure you are in a suitable position to initiate this profound deliverance. Set yourself apart. What does that mean? It means that there will be nothing Satan can accuse you of. The Bible says in Jeremiah 31:29,

In those days, people would no longer say, 'The parents have eaten sour grapes, and the children's teeth are set on edge."

Deep deliverance requires total submission to God; if there is still a trace of resistance to submit in you, eliminate it before entering this session of deep deliverance.

Chapter 7:
Closer to The Secret Place

Fasting Spiritual and Physical benefits;

Spiritually; Fasting is a deeply significant spiritual discipline with a range of sacred purposes, frequently undertaken in conjunction with prayer to cultivate a more profound communion with God. It serves as a means of seeking divine guidance, enabling individuals to attune their hearts more clearly to God's voice and discern His will with greater clarity. Furthermore, fasting functions as a solemn act of repentance an outward manifestation of an inward turning away from sin and a renewed commitment to righteousness. The voluntary abstention from food symbolizes a posture of humility and a conscious acknowledgment of human dependence upon God's sovereignty and provision.

This spiritual exercise also enhances the efficacy of prayer, sharpening one's spiritual focus and fostering a deeper intimacy with the divine. Fasting strengthens believers in their resistance to temptation, as exemplified by Christ during His forty days in the wilderness, thereby emphasizing the necessity of self-discipline in the face of spiritual trials. It is likewise employed as a form of preparation for ministry, an appeal for divine protection or deliverance, and a heartfelt expression of concern for the advancement of God's kingdom.

Moreover, fasting may serve as a tangible demonstration of compassion through acts of service to those in need, aligning one's actions with the values of mercy and justice. In times of mourning or national crisis, it becomes a powerful vehicle for expressing grief and lamentation. In all these ways, fasting emerges as a comprehensive spiritual practice that integrates the mind, body, and soul in submission to God's will and in pursuit of His purposes.

Physically; Fasting offers several physical benefits that contribute to overall health and well-being. One of the most notable advantages is improved metabolic health. By giving the digestive system a break, fasting allows the body to regulate insulin levels more effectively, enhancing insulin sensitivity and reducing the risk of type 2 diabetes. It also promotes fat burning by encouraging the body to use stored fat as a primary source of energy, which can support weight loss and improve body composition. Additionally, fasting triggers a process called autophagy, where the body cleans out damaged cells and regenerates healthier ones, potentially reducing the risk of chronic diseases such as cancer and Alzheimer's. Fasting has also been shown to lower inflammation, improve heart health by reducing blood pressure and cholesterol levels, and support better digestion by allowing the gastrointestinal system to rest and reset. Moreover, many individuals report increased mental clarity and energy during fasting periods, as the body is not constantly focused on digestion. Overall, when practiced safely and appropriately, fasting can be a powerful tool to enhance physical health and longevity.

Overall, the more you fast and draw closer to God, the more you hear His voice and receive direction. When you eat, all the blood vessels and nerves in your body concentrate on your stomach for digestion and for the body's mechanisms to take place. So, they shift their focus from your brain and concentrate on the stomach to ensure that the regular mechanism of food digestion is taking place. When you fast, all the best vessels that are concentrating on food digestion focus on your brain instead. This way, you find yourself hungry but mentally alert, and as you pray, you can easily hear the Lord—His voice becomes even more distinct. You will notice that the moment you begin fasting, you experience a constant revelation of the Word of God as you read it; dreams will become more apparent, and God will reveal many things to you.

That's why fasting is an essential preparation for a child of God. You must know that the season you are entering now is unlike any other you have experienced in your entire life. In other words, you're taking on another kingdom. You need to prepare mentally and physically.

> *Isaiah 47:1: Come down, and sit in the dust, O virgin daughter of Babylon, sit on the ground: there is no throne, O daughter of the Chaldeans: for thou shalt no more be called tender and delicate.*

You set yourself apart because family members and friends could distract you during this process. Satan will bring people who make sure they cause destruction and distortion of the season. It could be the spouse, children, or friends. Therefore, you must be very careful during this season. However, since you already have this understanding in mind, nothing can take you off track, regardless of what comes. You handle it accordingly, sticking to the assignment. You know it is the enemy who is trying to do this, and you have made up your mind not to pay attention to any distractions. That's what it means. Prepare; stay in the secret place more often. How do you spend more time in the secret place?

Stay close to God. Stay prayed on. Do more confession, renunciation, and repentance, and ask for cleansing of yourself and the family tree as the foundation.

***John 17:19: "And for their sake I consecrate
myself, that they also may be sanctified in truth."***

Consecrate yourself for the cleansing of every member
of your family tree. It is God who gives you the grace even
to do that. God is looking for such people. The Bible says
the harvest is plentiful, but the workers are few.

As you consecrate yourself, you are enveloped with the
presence of God, and you attract angels of God. You keep
yourself surrounded and soaked in the blood of Jesus. The
Bible says, *'Build a wall of fire around my city.* 'Your
dwelling is a no-fly zone; no unclean spirits, monitoring
spirits, evil personalities, demons, spells, or enchantment are
allowed. All must go in the name of Jesus, because, though
you are in this world, you are also in the secret place. At this
point, you are no longer a natural person; you are operating
in the realm of the supernatural. The Bible says,

***Ephesians 5:18: "Do not get drunk with wine, for
that is debauchery, but be filled with the Spirit."***

This is the point where you begin to operate from a
different realm, and those surrounding you can attest that
there is a distinct power within you, a different anointing that
is not a natural power. The Bible says *He makes His angels
wind and His ministers flames of fire.* Your life is not your
own; He orders your steps. The jealousy of God is hedging
you. Angels of God encompass you all the time. And now
you can begin that journey of deep deliverance because *deep
calleth unto deep.* It is a journey that you must take with a
profound understanding and a clear mind. When you begin
this kind of thing, you also must know that they'll project
anything. Astrologers will *astro-project* in your life; it's like
part of monitoring your spirit, so make sure to pray every
day a prayer against them that says, *"I cut the silver cord of*

astro-projection." Astro-project your family, children, spouse, business, ministry, premature death, sacrifice, health, career, promotion, and destiny; take authority in the name of Jesus and cut the silver cord of astro-projection. Many are still unaware of the spiritual realm; they think things are just happening, and they say it's terrible luck when, in fact, it's an *astro-project*.

You are being looked at; you are haunted; you are being monitored. They will do everything possible to stop you by sending the monitoring spirits. All this is to interrupt what God is trying to do with your life. Therefore, you must be very careful not to blend in with the surroundings, as anyone can be an agent of darkness and take you down at any time. Take communion during this season if you can, to intercept the works of the evil one every single day in the name of Jesus. Call upon the blood of Jesus to speak for you because it speaks better than the blood of Abel.

Do not be Ignorant of the Devices of the Crafty.

Don't remain ignorant or walk naked; stay covered and protected by the presence of God and the full armor of God. At this point in the journey, there's a target on your back live or dead. If they can't get you, they will hunt your family and your children. If they can't get your children, they'll go to your wife; if they can't get you a wife, they'll go to your husband. If they can't get any of you, they have to go to your sibling or your parents, even to your properties, because it is a battle, and they want to make sure they hurt you. You must call everyone connected to you by bloodline, those whom you can remember, and ensure that you immerse them in the blood of Jesus. You put on the whole armor of God for all of them: a helmet of salvation, a breastplate of righteousness, a belt of truth, sandals of the gospel of peace, a shield of faith, and a sword of the Spirit. Therefore, you must do everything possible with the help of the Holy Spirit.

> **Psalm 66:12: Thou hast caused men to ride over our heads; we went through fire and through water: but thou broughtest us out into a wealthy place."**

God is watching as you go through this fire. So, instead of complaining, you keep pushing. You are a watchman, a warrior, you carry a generational scepter. You will come out victorious. For gold to be gold, it must undergo refining by fire. The Bible says, *'He who sits in heaven shall laugh.'* God is happy to see you pushing. As you push, you are navigating through the heavens to reach our Father in heaven, where you can sit with Jesus Christ at the right hand of the Father in the heavenly places, far above the powers of darkness and the rulers of this world, far above principalities and dominions.

Deep battle, why deep battle?

Because the root is deep, it has remained untouched for so long; it has generated all the roots it can. To tackle these roots, you also need to be thorough. Many of us don't have time for the deep; that's why generations are wasted right before our eyes. Churches are wasted right before our eyes. Satanic priests rule the Church that God has given to us on the altar; servants in the Church of God are satanic children; great-spiritual father are falling in good numbers ending their term in service with great shame because they have compromised and mixed themselves with the children of the devil, their anointing has been corrupted. This is a powerful lesson for all anointed vessels of God. This is not how you want to end your service in the Kingdom of God. We must be careful about whom we associate with. Even if they come bearing a large seed, it may be nothing more than an attempt to corrupt your anointing and exchange it, leaving you in shame and disgrace. That's why it's time for a deep dive into the depths. This is how the generational commanders are raised. Thank God for the understanding, knowledge, and wisdom. We call it the University of Heaven right here on Earth.

The Holy Spirit is teaching us. The Holy Spirit is revealing these secrets of the satanic kingdom through people who are being delivered and were serving the satanic kingdom. I salute every deliverance minister, for this is a total sacrifice. So, the foundational root is touched and shaken. Suppose we have clean roots in the foundation. In that case, we will undoubtedly have a clean, straight family, and we will automatically have people in the Church of God who know what God wants and how to keep His commandments, staying in purity, holiness, and righteousness. People who can represent the Kingdom of God right here on earth.

The single foundation roots have gone deeper because no one knew what to do or how to go about it in that first generation. The root is sin, and what is needed here is confession and renouncing of sin in the 1st generation, like sorcery, divination, bloodshed, adultery, fornication, and witchcraft.

That one root went untouched, and in the second generation, it's producing many more, even bitter roots. Here, confession and renouncing of transgression in 2nd-generation rebellion, idolatry, bitterness, injustice, impurity, immorality, and greed are required. In the second generation, those many roots are bathing even more routes and are manifesting as inequity in the third generation, which presents as afflictions of all kinds, for example, asking for cleansing of afflictions in the third generation like madness, confusion, insanity, barrenness, poverty, slavery, infirmities, death, addiction, shame, reproach, oppression, vanity, blindness, rejection, demonic oppression, violence, abuse, sorrow, captivity, defilement, and premature death.

So, something that started as one root in the first generation, due to sin, has become more profound in the second generation, and it has evolved into transgression —a more severe form of evil. In the third generation, it has become a state of inequity, accompanied by numerous afflictions. If we all ask, how did we even get here? One is a lack of knowledge. The second is laziness, wanting a quick fix in church. The third is allowing too many motivational speakers in church, which makes people forget their problems for a second, and featuring entertainers of the Word of God on the altar. Also, destroying deliverance Ministers, all this is Satan wanting to swallow deliverance so that people will not come to the truth of their destroyed foundation.

Additionally, the Church has lost its prophetic watchmen and intercessors. The Church is no longer a house of prayer but has become a den of robbers; people are there to make profits, entertain, and motivate, rather than to worship. No rebuke, no repentance, no conviction by the Holy Spirit, because people are often disconnected from the Holy Spirit in many churches. This is evident in the diluted gospel they present to their members, the superficiality of the church's attire, and the prevalence of sin within the church. It is hell in the church of Christ right here on earth. And no one wants to speak about it. Sheep are sent to hell by shepherds in good numbers every single day. God is watching! Souls are crying, tormented, looking for help, but no one has a solution.

If the foundations are destroyed, what can a righteous person do?

If the foundation of the family is destroyed, the family is compromised; if the family is compromised, the Church is also compromised. Church worshipers are trained by Satan. The Bible says

> *1 Corinthians 15:33: Be not deceived: evil communications corrupt good manners.*

Where does the solution come from?

This is the time we need to run to;

> *2 Chronicles 7:14: If my people, who are called by my name, will humble themselves and pray and seek my face and turn from their wicked ways, then I will hear from heaven, and I will forgive their sin and will heal their land.*

And this is the perfect time and season to run to God, humble ourselves, and cry together as a church and a nation. Globally, it is all possible. God is paying closer attention to every detail of our time and season. Each of us has an assignment to fulfill in the Kingdom of God. If you are truly for Christ, ask God; He will reveal your assignment to you. I counsel you not to be a spectator in the house of the Lord. What are you called to? Ask the Almighty to reveal to you. This is also another way to keep your account active in the storehouse of heaven. When you call on God, it is easy to pull out your file and find that you were committed to His Kingdom. Everything you do in your account in heaven is noticed and recorded.

FOUNDATIONAL ROOT.

The root of sin, transgression, and iniquity has gone deeper; it started with children. The root has grandchildren; the root has great-grandchildren spreading even to the neighbors. And no one is ready to uproot it. No one is ready to face the Lord and ask what to do, for many are watching Satan sift one family after the other. We have become a disobedient generation, moreover, tuned to Satan for solutions that do not require purity or repentance. That's why you have a satanic minister on the altar preaching Jesus yet in deep sin, sending people to hell every single day. Satanic priests on the altar demonstrating powers on the people of God, while the source of power is Satan. They are sorcerers, warlocks, and wizards on the altar of the Lord Jesus Christ. I beg you to take good care of your soul; don't be careless, for God is still in need of your soul. The problem we face today as a church is a lack of obedience. Everything we need we ask from God is clothed in obedience.

OBEDIENCE;

Obedience is the act of willingly following instructions or commands from an authority, done with a respectful and trusting attitude. In a spiritual context, it means submitting to God's will, obeying His Word, and living according to His commandments. In the Bible, obedience reflects love and faith in God, as shown in the example of Abraham. It leads to blessings, protection, and spiritual growth, while disobedience can bring negative consequences. As Jesus said in John 14:15, "If you love Me, keep My commandments," highlighting that true obedience flows from a loving relationship with God.

Obedience, it means sitting at the feet of Jesus so that you can be taught the things of God and follow the path of

Christ and His commandments. The deliverance we seek is found in obedience; healing is achieved through obedience; freedom, wealth, rest, peace, and joy are all found in obedience. Obedience is what will keep your covenant with Christ and make your journey of salvation smooth. It's up to us to choose what we want. If we choose disobedience instead, the hand of God is lifted off from us, and that is when the enemy comes in like a flood.

What happened here?

The Bible says;

> **1 Corinthians 5:5: "Hand this man over to Satan for the destruction of the flesh, so that his spirit may be saved on the day of the Lord Jesus."**

God is still God; He is still on the throne. Until we return to our senses, we will come back to our Father, and He is ready to receive us back with love, restoring our families, our children, our church, and our nation.

Let us seek the Lord; He is still found, but it will require us to sit down and pay attention to Him only. Those who keep running from one church to the other are not seeking God; they are seeking the Man of God. And the enemy has thrown these kinds of people into churches of dragons, Baphomet, and marine churches, as well as water churches. It's like the enemy keeps sending them more for destruction. They are seeking deliverance due to the trouble they are in, but deliverance does not come simply by touching. Deliverance comes from the Lord, and the Bible says that deliverance is the bread of the children. For God to give you His deliverance, you must sit and seek Him, and Him alone. What you perceive as an affliction in your life, behind it lies sin, transgression, inequity, disobedience, which require you to sit down and seek deliverance through confession, renunciation, and repentance.

> ***Mathew 5:25:*** *"Settle matters quickly with your adversary who is taking you to court. Do it while you are still together on the way, or your adversary may hand you over to the judge, and the judge may hand you over to the officer, and you may be thrown into prison.*

Many of us have ignored the word of God, and that's how the enemy throws us into prison because of our stiff necks, for the word of God is clear and settled. Examples of prisons that the enemy has thrown us into are: divorce, addiction, sickness, infirmities, witchcraft, evil attacks, marital contention, death, failure, pain, sorrow, limitation, retrogression, homosexuality, lesbianism, gays, etc. God is watching until we return to Him and Him alone.

Chapter 8:
Detailed Deliverance

Deliverance is like an onion; the more you peel back from the top, the deeper you go inside. Let me say that the top was perhaps two thousand years ago, and that's the one that's sitting there, just waiting for anyone to uproot it and throw it into the fire, because it's already tired now. If you go to the middle of the onion, the middle is the one that is bothering you because it's strong, powerful, and energizing the covenant. When you go to the bottom of the onion, that's the fresh onion, a baby onion, which means more young foundational roots are growing. So, this is what it means when I tell you the root has babies, grandchildren, and great-grandchildren. Foundational deep deliverance requires you to sit down and connect with God for total and complete deliverance. You will not be delivered if you can't sit down. The men of God can touch you; you will find temporary relief. If your case involves foundational deliverance, your route is to pursue deliverance through intercessory prayers, and that's what this entire book explains. In our case, we offer intercessory and sacrificial prophetic prayers every day at midnight. That's how you uproot deep foundation roots, foundational deliverance.

Some deliverance can be more straightforward if someone has already done foundational, deep-rooted deliverance within the family. However, the more profound deliverance, the deep things we are talking about, involves strongmen and strongholds that have been present for ages, rooted in family foundations; these will require you to sit down and undertake a serious process of following proper deliverance under proper direction through intercessory prayers. God is disciplining us to learn how to sit in His presence and be delivered.

Why do you need to sit down?

God has selected you to deliver many souls behind you. And if you are going to read this book and hear this message, it means you are the one God is interested in; He is counting on you in some way. Somewhere, He has carefully examined you and watched over you, and you are now qualified to take on this divine assignment. God is ready to empower you and give you the knowledge that you need to carry on this assignment. If you are reading this book for a reason, you need to understand why you are reading it in the first place. Because this is not like any other message, it will draw you into your divine calling. It is God who has sent you here, not by coincidence. God is speaking loud and clear: *You are the one I need for your family, your church, your generation, your nation, and your territory.* Stop running away like Jonah.

You are only wasting your time running; know that you will end up making a U-turn just like Jonah. Running away will only make you weary and tired, causing more destruction and confusion. Running away will only continue to derail your divine call— not just any call, but that divine call you have left behind for a long time. Jonah tried to run away from a divine call; now he is destroying people's property, and the ship is sinking. It doesn't matter how you delay; it doesn't matter how you run away; the Eye of God will still locate you until you do His assignment. Even after Jonah was thrown into the sea, the sea refused to kill Jonah; the sea creatures also declined to eat Jonah. Jonah wrestled with God and nature. However, the divine assignment was in Nineveh, and only Jonah, among all the people God created, was tasked with fulfilling it.

Could this be you? Is it just the name and the time that have changed? Yes, I was also Jonah. I don't know about you. The fish swallowed Jonah and then brought him safely to dry land, spitting him out right on the coast of the sea. Jonah had to surrender because he realized whatever he was trying to do was not working. Jonah, that's how he answered the call. Today, for God to pay attention to mankind, He must forcefully take us through Jonah's experience, each one of us having a unique experience. I don't know what your Jonah's experience is, but if you see me humbling myself before the Lord, it's because I have had my own Jonah experience, and I am here fearfully to answer the call of the Most High God, Yahweh. The Jonah experience I had was personal, so please don't judge me; it's the one that motivates me to go above and beyond in matters of God.

God gives you a second chance if you are one of the Jonahs. It was at the second chance that Jonah got it right. God gives us a second chance to families, churches, governments, and nations. God is very patient with us. But understand the time and the season so that you will not miss out again on what God wants and what He is doing. This time, you will do the right thing so that the Ninevites can be saved from the anguish of God, and God can take His glory.

You are the chosen one to speak the mind of God, to extend the voice of God, and not just to dilute the message of God to make people feel good, so you can keep your church filled with numbers, but with zero fear for the Lord and zero repentance. No, you must deliver the message exactly as the Lord says it. It's not about the number of people in your church anymore; it is about where you are directing these innocent souls. It's about diluting the gospel, manipulating and twisting scriptures, and diverting the people of God.

When God sends a message to His people, He also prepares them. Jonah delivered the message with ease, and it was received and acted upon. The land and the people were saved because Jonah did not dilute the message. The country and the land were thoroughly restored. That is our God.

Who qualifies to deliver the people of God?

If you are not fully delivered, the enemy will not allow you to fully deliver what God wants you to give to His people. The subject of deliverance is for everyone who has never done deliverance, regardless of title or rank. Denying deliverance is agreeing to permanently stay in bondage, which will affect the children and the unborn generation. It is so spiritual. You can live, you can work hard as you want, as long as there is a legal right somewhere, the enemy will wait for you at the point of breaking through; the point of your rising is when the enemy strikes to make sure you will never rise. Not only that, but also continuous attacks on family members, children, spouse, ministry, business, career, health, divorce, finances. Remember, Satan will not harass you unless there is a legal right, and Satan is a master of law; he knows where to stop you just because you have ignored the legal covenant, whether in the spirit or physically. The covenant will hunt you wherever you go and whatever you do; we will hear one scandal after another, but physically, you are still a mighty man of God. Things must be done right and not ignored. If you ignore the covenant's scandals, shame, and afflictions, they will move from you to your children or grandchildren.

> *Psalms 11:3: If foundations are destroyed, what can a righteous do?*

That's why you find some of the mighty men of God are messing up, and you begin to wonder, are they truly faithful men of God? It's because they haven't been delivered. The covenant is seeking to have them stop; according to the covenant, they have trespassed and overstepped their jurisdiction. They are crossing boundaries they are not supposed to cross because the covenant is in place. The covenant is hunting them. The covenant calls them, so this is for everybody who has not been delivered: You can't continue hiding under Jesus' name. You need to do the right thing for God to be able to use you fully. The Bible says there is no confusion where the spirit of God is.

If you are not delivered, you are limited in so many things, because you are still under satanic control. There are still unattended legal rights. Customary daily prayers won't remove these legal covenants; they must be accompanied by confession, repentance, renunciation, and a request for cleansing. If you ignore this, you will see yourself supporting unbiblical things because they control you; they influence your thoughts and actions. That is why sin has become the new normal on the pulpit. They also have verses to justify their sin at the altar. A powerful man of God associates with an evil man; the Bible says that bad company corrupts good morals.

When you are fully surrendered, you'll become a new creature. God will take complete control of you, and you'll begin to fear the Lord, for the fear of the Lord is the beginning of wisdom. Wisdom takes control of your words; your communication and actions are full of wisdom. Today, we have many behind the pulpit with zero wisdom or knowledge of the Lord and zero fear of the Lord. This is because the ministry has become a business. You sow a big seed; the next thing they call you to lay hands on you and give you a microphone. That is how cheap ministries have become. That is how easy it has been for Satan to penetrate the Church.

God is calling many into deliverance to take them to higher heights and stay there, but He cannot take them to higher heights until they address the flaws in their foundation. Otherwise, whatever they have gotten outside the will of God will not last long, whether it is spiritual gifts or not. God is exposing these falsehoods. Those who got their spiritual knowledge from Satan are sorcerers and diviners behind the pulpit using the name Jesus to shame the name of the Lord Jesus and to harvest souls for Satan. God is highly exposing them, and they will pay back for the evil they have done and the souls they have led astray. All their gimmicks are coming to an end; God is stepping in now to defend His name. So those are deep battles. And why are they powerful? Because of covenants, the Bible says:

> ***Deuteronomy 5:9: You shall not bow down to them or worship them; for I, the Lord your God, am a jealous God, punishing the children for the sin of the parents to the third and fourth generation of those who hate me, 10 but showing love to a thousand generations of those who love me and keep my commandments.***

Who is nurturing the evil covenant in my foundation?

Covenants will not survive if no one is nurturing them by making sacrifices. Who is nurturing the covenant? It could be a satanic priest or priestess connected to you, an aunt, an uncle, a parent, or whoever received the septa and carried on this satanic assignment for the family tree. That is why the covenant from five hundred years ago still looks alive. The more you try to do the work of God, the more it seems like they are overpowering you, they are pulling you even though you don't see who is pulling. That's why you are struggling so much in ministry, in family, and financially, because they know once everything sits well with you, you will overturn their kingdom upside down, overthrow them, and bring the kingdom of light into the foundation. So, they will deal with you. Even though you said you were born again, there is still a covenant from past generations that was not renounced.

God is the just judge. It is just like our Father in heaven; the covenant with Jesus is the legal covenant. So, if the powers of darkness have a legal covenant on your family, you cannot just say, *I have received Jesus, and everything is done*. No, that's a ticket you carry. You carry the blood of Jesus now. You go and confront Satan. *Why are you still in my family? Jesus died for me; I am a conqueror; why are you still in my foundation? Why are you still following me? Why are you still scattering things around here? I have Jesus. I have light; I bring light now*. You begin to command every darkness to depart, for light cometh; darkness comprehended it not! And Jesus came to destroy the works of the enemy. You are born again, a new creature, and the former is gone.

After you confess, repent, and renounce, you can ask for cleansing from the Lord. You can safely begin to take authority over the dark kingdom, commanding things because you can't command something that has authority over you, which is what many of us have been doing. Once you take authority, God will back up your word, and you will begin seeing those situations disappear.

God is raising a remnant of an army that understands what they need to do now. The Bible says that *from the days of John the Baptist up until now, the Kingdom of heaven suffered violence, and the violent are taking it by force.* What are you doing? What do you want to take? What they have taken, stolen, and exchanged. Because the Bible says you will recover the former, the present, and the latter simultaneously. But God will need a vessel ready to be used by Him, a vessel that understands He is holy. So, for you to be helped by God, that chosen vessel has to yield itself to holiness. And that vessel is you. God will help you; He will do what He said He will do. You can't afford to continue calling on the name of Jesus only to be put to shame, or your life is crumbling left and right. The Bible says in Isaiah 45:19, *I did not call the house of Jacob to seek me in vain.*

But if the foundation is faulty, carry the blood of Jesus and do the right thing. That's how God can come through for you quickly. You have done all you know how to do: fasted, prayed. When you see that the legal rights are persistent, that means Satan is trespassing. You need to drag them to the Courts of Heaven.

As a believer, you are living in the supernatural even though you are on this earth, and your life is supernatural. If things are not panning out, an enemy is doing that. Every enemy in your life has a legal right. However, God also has a legal right to you after you have received salvation and are living according to God's commandments. So, if you are saved and the enemy oppresses you, drag them to the court of heaven. God will do the right thing here, for He is a just judge. The Bible says:

> **Daniel 7:10: A river of fire was flowing, coming out from before him. Thousands upon thousands attended him; ten thousand times ten thousand stood before him. The court was seated, and the books were open.**

Praise be to God! Now, why are books open? The books are opened for your lawyer, the great and just judge, the advocate, our Jesus Christ of Nazareth. The blood of Jesus is there to defend you. Now, when you go there, why is the book open? They are looking into your matter. Why is this stubbornness? What could be the problem? Why are you not receiving a release? Now, when you go to heaven's courts, God will ask why your matter is not settled. The courts of heaven look just like regular courts here on Earth. Eventually, God will grant you a verdict. The Bible says that when the thief is caught, he shall return sevenfold of what he has stolen. As you conduct your investigation, you are confident that the thief must be caught and brought to justice. It is time for a sevenfold restoration; it is time for restoration with compassion. Also, the promise in the Bible to restore what the palmerworm and locust have eaten in the name of Jesus, because now you have broken loose from every satanic connection. The shackle is broken, the cord is broken, and the cage is broken; you are officially out of the bondage, in the name of Jesus.

My job is to ensure that my children will not have to go through this kind of battle. I say no; I will go ahead and pursue the enemy until I stop Satan in the name of Jesus Christ of Nazareth. Our God is a just judge. A verdict is rendered from the courts of heaven to me and my family. It's beautiful to hear it from the mouth of God himself in the courts of heaven. Praise be to God hallelujah! salvation, power and glory belong to our God! hallelujah!

I'm building on this strong rock, for the Bible says, *Upon this rock, I shall build a Church, and the gates of hell shall not prevail.* This is the release of my foundation. I am bold enough to stand and speak out in any situation or face any foundation battles. The Bible says, *Submit to the Lord, and resist the devil, and he shall flee from you.* I submitted it to my tiny mind. In my small understanding, I knew if I could cling close to this God, He would help me. I resisted the devil, and the devil, eventually the enemy, fled from me, my children, and my foundation. Remember, most want to resist the devil without submitting fully to the Lord God Almighty. That's why many of our churches appear powerless. Great men and great women of God are powerless but full of the word of God. For this generation to believe, there must be the word of God, which has power. The Bible says that where the word of the King is, there is power. And when you submit totally to the Lord, He will give you just that; you don't have to go to seek from other gods.

Deep deliverance cleans the bloodline, and a new, clean generation has recovered. Now, deliverance is one thing, but maintaining deliverance is another. Stay in the supernatural in the secret place where you will maintain what you have been delivered from, and remain connected to the source where you read the word and pray. That is how your deliverance can be permanent. This is what we call true deliverance. Everything you have attained from the place of prayer after you have done your deliverance, you must maintain it with prayer. One way to determine if someone has undergone deliverance is by the fear of God that is upon them and their commitment to maintaining obedience, righteousness, purity and holiness.

SUBMISSION

"Throughout this text, we have been talking about submission. But what exactly is the submission we are referring to? James 4:7 says, 'Therefore submit to God. Resist the devil, and he will flee from you.'

Salvation is another word for deliverance, A delivered man pursues a life of brokenness and submission., Where there is brokenness in a man, there is submission. The Church of Christ today is on the path to backsliding because there is no brokenness, and there is no submission.

In such a state, this is why God said, "I looked for someone among them who would stand in the gap." When none could be found, He said, "I will come to judge and make war. "Revelation 19:11.

For over a thousand years, every time the Church grew cold, God raised up a man or a people who became uncomfortable with the status quo and began to seek the truth. I believe that people are you and me called to stand out, speak the truth, and declare the Word of God.

Today, there are too many games and politics in the Church. The Bible says, "Come out from among them," and, "Wake up, O sleeper!" This reveals two kinds of believers: those who are asleep and those who are awake.

Sleeping believers no longer repent, no longer forgive, and no longer praise. Many have forsaken the foundation and that is why so many now turn to extras, such as water, oil, or handkerchiefs, turning them into idols. It's like someone eating dessert and forgetting the main course, which contains all the nourishment. The Church is eating only desert; the main course of the menu is slowly departing from the altar.

Many churches now believe that the anointing is simply prophesying or causing people to fall to the ground. Because the foundation has been abandoned, there is a rise in practices of sorcery, witchcraft and divination, all in the name of deliverance. The Church must return to its true foundation: the Holy Spirit, the blood of Jesus, and the Word of Truth.

Many are so spiritual they can see in the spirit and prophecy yet they miss the foundation of Christ. So, what is the foundation? Love. In 1 Corinthians 13:1–8, the Apostle Paul teaches that no matter how gifted or self-sacrificing a person is, without love, it is all meaningless. He describes love as patient, kind, humble, forgiving, and enduring. Unlike spiritual gifts such as prophecy, speaking in tongues, or knowledge which are temporary, love is eternal and never fails. True completeness will come one day, but only love remains forever.

Paul said, "I will show you the more excellent way." Today, we often focus on gifts, power, and demonstrations but not on the perfect way, which is the foundation. Even without prophecy or spiritual gifts, you can still make it to heaven. The spiritualism of today has led many into deep deception, and in some cases, even the initiation of children because people are trying to find solutions outside of God. Everything else may perish, but what will remain is the Word of God His truth. All of this happens because, as believers, we have not obeyed the call to personal consecration or committed to finishing the journey of our salvation with God.

Your deliverance and maintaining your deliverance come through total submission to God. Discern the spirits, because today we have magicians who are called pastors, prophets, and apostles. God is investigating, exposing and punishing the Church in the area we often call "miracles," because many of the so-called miracles today are nothing more than mind games.

Many people have been "delivered" by a magician using anointed oil, holy stones, handkerchief, water, or soil. That is not deliverance it is divination, idolatry, and witchcraft.

Anything you do that goes against the Word of God is idolatry and sorcery.

When people fall down under a false spirit, it is often a spirit of darkness manipulating people's minds making them believe they have had a real experience with God, only to waste their lives in deception and spiritual darkness.

The call God is giving you is to walk in the journey of submission, Submit to God. That is the first and most vital stage.

Do You submit to God? How do you know you are truly submitting to God?

It is in five stages;

1. Brokenness

It all begins with brokenness. It is through brokenness that God ushers you into the next stage.

2. Abiding

After brokenness comes abiding in God. Jesus said in John 15:5: *"I am the vine; you are the branches. Whoever abides in me and I in him, he it is that bears much fruit, for apart from me you can do nothing."*

To abide is to remain in His love, remain in His Word. As you learn to abide, the Lord calls you into stillness. In Matthew 22:44, it is written: *"The Lord said to my Lord, 'Sit at my right hand until I make your enemies your footstool.'"*

Sit in the presence of God. Read your Bible. Wait upon the Lord and let His Word work within you. In this generation, believers are often restless, running here and there, saying, *"The Lord told me to go to the prophet,"* or *"The Lord told me to sow a seed."* But often, that is not the Spirit of God speaking, it is the flesh.

I pray that the Holy Spirit will arrest you, detain you at the feet of Jesus, so you can consecrate yourself and learn how to abide in the Word of God. A time is coming when you will testify, *"I am no longer deceived. I am sitting at the feet of Jesus, learning to abide in Christ."*

You are now practicing how to remain in the presence of God. And abiding brings peace, because His presence is undeniable.

3. Sanctification

As you continue to abide, the Lord begins the work of sanctifying you cleansing, refining, transforming you before He can glorify you.

4. Glorification

At this stage you are being made perfect by Him spiritually and physically so that you can dwell eternally in His presence, reflecting His holiness and glory.

After sanctification comes glorification. Then you enter into;

5. Oneness with the Lord

At this stage, your submission is complete. Oneness means there is no longer a separation between you and God. You are crucified with Christ, you are dead to self, and alive in Him. You no longer question God. The cross has dealt with your flesh. You are now glorified in Him, walking in unity with His Spirit.

Many have not yet reached this stage, but **every day I press in**, believing that one day, by His grace, I will.

Be encouraged.

Do not stop. Do not be deceived. Keep seeking. Keep growing. This is a journey a walk of submission with the Lord.

In this season especially, I pray that you continue surrendering. I pray that you keep yielding to the Holy Spirit. The days we are in and what is ahead require you to be fully aligned with the will of God. Let Him bring you into His likeness so you may fully bear His image.

Now is the time to be serious with God.

Tell Him: *"Lord, I am hungry for the truth. I want to know You. My heart longs for Your presence."*

Prayer Points

1. ***Total Surrender to God's Will***

   Lord Jesus, I belong to You. I surrender fully have Your way in my life. Shape me, lead me, and do with me as You will. Let my life reflect Your purpose and glory.

2. ***Love and Compassion to Be an Answer***

   Father, teach me to love like You love. Fill my heart with compassion, that I may be an answer to someone's cry. Make me a vessel of healing, peace, and hope in a broken world.

3. ***Grace to Abide and Surrender***

   Holy Spirit, teach me to abide in Christ. Let Your love dwell richly in me. I surrender my thoughts, my will, and my desires let me remain rooted in You, drawing life from Your presence.

4. ***Healing, Deliverance, and Restoration***

   Lord, I lift up every heart that has been afflicted whether in body, soul, or spirit. As they declare, "I am Yours," let Your healing power flow. Release deliverance, restore what was lost, and establish peace in their lives.

5. **Truth and Purity in the Church**

O God, send Your truth like fire into Your Church. Expose every hidden agenda, manipulation, and deception. Purify the altar. Raise up a remnant of truth-bearers who walk in holiness and fear of the Lord.

You are the generation that must come to a place of brokenness, so that God can work freely through you.

Brokenness means surrender allowing God full access to your heart, your plans, and your life. When you are broken before the Lord, He can shape you, mold you, and move through you without resistance.

After brokenness comes abiding a season of waiting upon the Lord. It is in the place of abiding that God begins to discipline you, and that discipline leads to character development.

Your gift may open doors for you and take you to great places, but it is your character that will sustain you there.

Yes, the enemy will challenge what you have received. But when God has been working on your heart building character and teaching you to abide you will stand firm.

So, choose to be still. Choose to wait upon the Lord. As it is written in Isaiah 40:31: "But they who wait for the LORD shall renew their strength; they shall mount up with wings like eagles; they shall run and not be weary; they shall walk and not faint."

I choose to abide. I choose to remain in the place of consecration until God speaks. I choose to be different. This is the season for us all to abide in the Lord, and in that abiding, we will find our strength for the joy of the Lord is our strength.

Chapter 9:
Deliverance Phases

The deliverance journey I have taken; I have discovered that there are phases of deliverance; this is just my own experience, which God guided me through as I underwent my deep foundation deliverance.

Phase One

Powers are so vicious and tormenting, to the point you can't even sleep. You wake up mentally and physically drained, not knowing what you did. I have heard some people say they have dreams of farming all night on their uncle's farm or carrying and transporting things from one place to another. God is revealing so many things to the children of God. Otherwise, it is not easy to learn these things, for there is no school for this kind of education.

So, the first phase is characterized by a fear of deep, back-to-back battles. Powers that have been in control want to always remain in control. When you want to overtake them and take your throne back, they wage war against you. These powers have no problem with regular, religious Christians; they have a problem with those who have received knowledge and know the truth and wants to be free. This is the reason for the battle. Many have abandoned their dominion, authority, and territory because they fear being touched by the enemy. These powers like ignorant people; that's why the Bible says, *Do not be ignorant of the devices of the crafty.*

Ignorance has brought shame and pain to the children of God. It's ignorance that has led the children of God to attend church and return still in pain; it's ignorance that has caused children of God to read the Bible from Genesis to Revelation without a single encounter or lasting impact. That is why many have decided to settle for less and be satisfied with the little they have; they have abandoned their God-given destiny, abandoning the promises of God over them and leaving everything to Satan. When you experience deep foundation deliverance, you will know the enemy is real, and if God gives you the grace to go through it and be delivered, there is no way you can ever joke with the things of God. If you see any minister joking about the things of God, know they have not started their journey of deliverance.

The enemy will launch attacks at you- disappointment, evil voices, contention in the spirit realm, satanic kingdoms gathering to gang you, spirit spouses, snakes, water spirits, marine spirits, and witchcraft. To make sure you give up this deliverance journey. Because now they have realized that you are at a point of no return, no matter what they do to you.

James 4:7: Submit yourself then to God; resist the devil, and it shall flee from you.

Many of us want to do the second part of this verse- *resisting the devil will flee from you.* But the central part of this verse is the first part: *submit yourself to the Lord!* All who have undergone deep deliverance and achieved victory, this is the secret: they have submitted themselves fully to God. They have surrendered their lives to God and agreed to the life of purity, holiness, and righteousness, for He said, *Be ye holy, for I am holy.* You can't claim God to be your father if your ways are against purity, holiness, and righteousness. When you practice these things, you start to see the glory of God overtaking you because these are the things that attract God. So, before touching any foundation battle, you must examine yourself: are you in total submission to this God? In deep deliverance, the breakthrough is in submission. Through submission, the keys of deliverance are released to you, the secrets of deliverance are revealed to you, the power of God rests upon you, and you are given authority; angels are released for assistance.

Phase Two, Mind Attack;

The enemy will attack your mind. These are not only voices in your head. Submit yourself fully to the Lord and continue with your deliverance.

Your prayer point should be God giving you the grace to remain focused on the assignment, for this must be done and done well. That is why you need to pray for grace and strength to fight to the end. Children of God have been exploited by the kingdom of darkness and had everything taken and sold to satanic markets. But you will capture them back.

You are recovering the treasure box of your bloodline and your birthright. The powers, spirits, and personalities will move. However, they cannot survive without a human being, so they will always find someone else, as they have already grown accustomed to that luxurious life. That's why we need to educate many people about how to deliver and enforce the deliverance of their loved ones.

In this second phase, the enemy contends with your mind through dreams and strange nightly encounters like intercourse with spirits, being fed in the dream, swimming in the water, or finding yourself in the middle of a forest or the middle of strangers at night. Some people find themselves in the former houses they grew up in, naked or without shoes. That signals the presence of a spirit of retrogression, shame, and disgrace. You mustn't treat such dreams as inconsequential. Your prayer should be to bind the monitoring spirits with blindness. They launch such counterattacks against you because you have become a terror to their kingdom. You may often wake up so tired and helpless that you can't help it during this time. Questions of self-doubt and doubts of your salvation and relationship with God begin to swirl through your mind: *Am I really born again? Where is my God?*

It is a mind attack; the enemy is speaking in your head. That is why if you want to fight Satan and come out victorious, ignore what he is doing to you along the process. Satan is doing this to shift your focus and make you start complaining instead of continuing to push the battle. God is aware and watching; He wants you to go through this fire so that you will be as gold when you come out. For gold to be gold, it must pass through fire. God is watching and preparing your reward.

Through all this, what will bring quicker victory is consistency and discipline in what you are doing. Consistency is the one what will bring many children of God to their breakthrough. As you pursue, the enemy may leave, but not for long; they will stay close to see if you will continue with the same vigor, being consistent and disciplined. Imagine that when you fight and take rest, it's as if you have captured the territory. You go to rest, and the enemy comes back to reclaim that same territory.

> *Mathew 12:43-45: When a demon is cast out of a person, it roams around a dry region, looking for a place to rest, but never finds it. Then it says, 'I'll return to the house.*

That's why Phase Two is the contention phase. All you need is the strength of God, the spirit of God, and the power of God to get you through this phase.

What are the crucial things to do at this point? If you know you have some people who are very powerful in prayer, whether in a group or a friend, you can join them at midnight to neutralize the enemy's power. The Bible says *one can chase a thousand, and two can chase ten thousand.*

In this phase, I have discovered that, although God has the power to rescue you and take you out of the battle, he will not, so that you can be molded. If God had rescued me in the second phase, I wouldn't have known about the third phase. That is why I tell people that many of the things I was taught by the Holy Spirit. It is also important to pray at midnight because midnight is the enemy's operational period while men are sleeping, so he can steal, kill, and destroy. I pray that God will give you the grace to pray at midnight.

As I said earlier, God sometimes allows pain, torments, and anguish because He is molding you. His strength is yours, and He knows you will come through it so you can be used mightily as a vessel to liberate all those bound.

> ***Luke 22:31-32: Simon, Simon, Satan has asked to sift all of you as wheat. But I have prayed for you so that after you come out of it you can strengthen your brothers.***

You cannot say you are given a ministry to deliver what you have not been through. That's not possible. You have to go through it: You know the pain, the torment, and the sleepless night. So, when you are being raised as a deliverance minister, you know exactly what to do. Life is so spiritual indeed. Did the doctor's visit reveal triple-negative breast cancer? How did pancreatic cancer turn into a death sentence just on the spot? How did ovarian cancer turn to stage four in just three weeks after the initial diagnosis? Cancers are released like candies today; autism even has scientists confused. It is not a doctor's diagnosis; behind it, there is satanic manipulation for the gain of their kingdom. Child of God, wake up and take authority, for Satan is not playing and is not wasting any time. He is here to steal, kill, and destroy.

The heavenly school that the Lord has allowed you to experience here on earth is to teach others what reality is, rather than suggesting that negativity is the will of God. How about we change and say it is the will of Satan and begin to rebuke Satan immediately and cast him out in the name of Jesus? Don't you see Satan is stealing, killing, and destroying our lives? The Bible says,

Ephesians 5:14: Awake, O sleeper, rise up from the dead, and Christ will give you light.

For us to be awake, God lets Satan sift us; God prays for us to be able to withstand the battle so later on we can strengthen our breath as we go through these battles of life. God allows battles because many people who survive them end up as great soldiers and join the army of the Lord. God sends people to the fight whom He knows will not be casualties; they will bring victory so He can take the glory. If you are for God, you need to begin to be serious and always put on all the weapons of God; the devil is against your full commitment to this God. If you enter this deep foundation deliverance with all this understanding and knowledge, nothing will stop you, and nothing can take you back. You are in until you finish, and victory is guaranteed, and God will take the glory.,

When you enter this phase, your eyes are opened, and you can see things in the dream. Why are you dreaming about things? That means it is another step of growth in the spirit. Have you heard of people who never dream? Or dream but not remember? The enemy is shutting down their dreamland. Now, if you dream and remember, thanks to God, God is allowing you to deal with the dream. There is no useless dream. Dreams reveal what is in your foundation. God shows you, for example, snakes in your dreams. That means the serpentine kingdom is oppressing your life, so you will begin the journey of self-deliverance until you stop seeing this particular kingdom in the dream. Don't just brush it off and think it will go just like that; no, as long as you have not been delivered from it, it is still in your foundation, stealing, killing, and destroying. That is why God is showing you in the first place so you can uproot it, tear it down, destroy it, and overthrow it.

How do you know you are delivered from it? You'll not dream about it again. The kingdom you see in your dream means that your foundation worshiped it as their god. You don't know; that's why when you bring in your Jesus, they fight you because you are trespassing on the covenant, which is why there is a battle. You dream about mermaids; your foundation is also in the marine kingdom. Gather prayer points and videos, and pray until you stop seeing it again. You dream about spirit spouses, which means your foundation people are married to spirits, specifically water spirits. You look for prayer points for spirit spouses and video pray until you stop seeing them. This means the spirit spouses were to your parents and grandparents, meaning all former generations were afflicted by it, so you will be the first to take them down for the first time. And that is foundational deliverance from that particular kingdom.

Spirit spouses are jealous; people who are married to spirits have turbulence in their marriages, or they will not allow you to get married in a physical marriage. They cause the abortion of miracles and the miscarriage of babies; it is the demon to steal, kill, and destroy. I pray in the name of Jesus that God will give you the strength to set time apart and begin your deliverance. Deliverance takes time. No one can do it for you; you need someone to guide you through what to do and how to do it. As you pray and perform personal deliverance, you observe the progress until you eliminate all the kingdom influence over your bloodline.

When the contention phase is over, you have recovered most of the kingdoms, and even your dream life begins to change and make sense. Because they are losing your entire generation, your entire bloodline, and your entire foundation. So, that's why they have to work hard. For the first time, you can rest and sleep. You can sleep without having these terrible dreams.

Now, some divine dreams begin to come. God is moving you into the level of high discipline in the Kingdom of God. When you think of the battles you have fought, you can't afford to be cheap. You don't want to go back. Now, Phase two, the contention phase, is done.

Phase Three: Release And Authority

You'll begin to experience ease in both the physical and spiritual realms. You are in full control; no fear anymore. You can easily command things in a dream and begin to see agents taking off. How do you know? You begin to capture them in the dream. The same things you used to see in the dream and get scared of, now you are controlling and commanding them. Victory begins in the dream itself; your inner man is becoming so strong, and you cannot be manipulated. That's why the Bible says *command*. You are supposed to escape. The Bible says *my soul escapes just like the bird escapes outside the snare of the fowler*. All these Bible verses now they begin to make sense. When they have your soul, they are commanding negativity, poverty, disappointment, diseases, and afflictions. That's happening because they have something to hang on to. Now your soul cannot be manipulated anymore because it has been delivered, set free, and captured back; it is in your hands.

And now you can happily build the wall of fire. The Bible says, *Build the wall of fire around my city*, because Satan does not tire. He will keep trying. See, even if you're being delivered, have you kept the law of the Lord? Have you kept the principles of the Lord? Or have you fallen back? So, Satan will keep trying.

After this phase, you stop seeing yourself in these strange, demonic meetings. Instead, you begin to see the promises of God coming to pass. It is like you have discovered yourself; you are a new creation. You can start swimming in and enjoying the blessings of the Lord. God is pleased to release everything to you- He can bring the promises of Jeremiah 51:20 to pass, *You are my War Club, my weapon for battle. With you, I shatter nations. With you, I destroy kingdoms.*

Now, God's authority, dominion, grace, and favor begin to manifest fully because the enemy who stopped all this is officially destroyed in Jesus' name.

> *Luke 10:19:" I have given you authority to trample on snakes and the scorpion and. To overcome all of the power of the enemy, and nothing by any means shall harm you.*

Now you can start *trampling on* the kingdom of darkness because you have separated completely from them; you have the authority of Yahweh. You have uprooted, torn down, destroyed, and overthrown. Now, you can start building and planting what you want. No King of Persia can stop anything. You can carry the assignment to another level. The Lord is with you because your destiny is free for you to take on now.

Chapter 10:
Demonic Forces and Spiritual Powers in Dark Places.

Spirits in the dark kingdom are very real, but also difficult to understand and explain. This has given them room to multiply because many children of God could not come forward to describe what was happening; some didn't even want you to know. Some of them took things like they were expected. So, they multiply more when we keep hiding and not exposing them. And the thing we don't understand is where these things come from?

If you are not born again or if you are a lukewarm Christian or religious, you won't even see them or feel them. First, they regard you as one of theirs; none of your prayers will threaten them or shake their kingdom. So, they don't waste any time with people who don't pose a threat to them.

All hell breaks loose when one surrenders to Jesus. Suddenly, you see all five Kingdoms coming after you: witchcraft, marine, water spirits, serpentine (snakes), and animal. That means they had a door open, but they were functioning slowly from the hidden place behind the scenes. Also, there was not enough fire to make them uncomfortable and leave their hidden place; it is now where a serious born-again is discovering many things. You will notice them, and you will chase them away. Now, you have received salvation, and you become so vicious, and you want to begin to throw arrows and missiles, intense prayers, fasting, and all kinds of weapons. That is when they can no longer stand it. They begin to come in like a flood, to fight you. You need deep foundational deliverance. It is more than your neighbor bewitching you. It is more than my boss not liking me. It has now become a foundational matter. The Bible says that the Lord knows our minds and hearts. So, when God sees in your heart that you are eager to know, you are keen to find out, He will empower you and give you the necessary knowledge and understanding on this matter.

> *Ephesian 6:12: For we do not wrestle against flesh and blood, but against principalities, against powers, against the rulers of [a]the darkness of this age, against spiritual hosts of wickedness in the heavenly places.*

To learn the deep things of God, you need to be empowered. That's when you begin to see that you have a different kind of understanding. You begin to read more, to pray more, to fast more. The Holy Spirit enters and commands you from inside; your life is not yours anymore. Once God captures you, the first thing He will do is give you a mantle to pray and fast. Because in this journey of faith, prayer is everything. Dark kingdoms don't fear titles or fame; they fear someone who can pray with authority. The more you pray, the more you discover; the more you discover, the more you recover. The Holy Spirit will direct you to the materials of deliverance like, videos to watch and learn, the books, and the man or woman of God to listen to, and educate yourself.

I come from a strong Catholic background. My mom was a Roman Catholic nun, and my daddy was a Roman Catholic priest before they got out. Even after they left, they kept the practice of the Lord in our family. Yes, some of you understand how Roman Catholics can be bold in their actions, consistent, and disciplined, which is a very good lifestyle. So, I can tell you that we were a clan that prayed. My grandfather was a devout Catholic; when it was time for prayer, everyone had to obey and pray on their knees for one hour in the morning and evening.

But when I began to look around at the lives of many of my relatives, people around me that are connected to me my grandparents, my aunties, my uncles, and the young nephews and nieces, I could see that things are failing. There were many things happening that I didn't understand. I did not know the cause, and I believe so many people around our relatives were asking what was happening. For example, we had a premature death, a lot of premature deaths. Like I said earlier, there was the regular occurrence of premature deaths. There was also poverty: people are working so hard and are highly educated, even internationally outside the country in America, Asia and Europe. But there was poverty. Family members often work for a while, only to end up poor once they retire. Also, the issue of polygamy, idolatry, fornication, libel, disobedience to the Lord, rage, anger, curses, complex marital settlement, and divorce. But if you look around, you ask yourself: *What is happening? Is there a problem somewhere*? But that's what I realized as I was asking myself those questions: the spirit of God entered me. I wasn't asking myself; it was as if I were communicating, and I could hear. I can listen to the voice of God and receive direction on what to do and how to do it.

That's why you see all these verses coming on. But then the Lord sent a strange person into my life, the one who led me to Christ. I was born again. After I was born again, this person gave me the Bible, and I became curious and committed to reading it. While reading the Bible, the Lord spoke to and answered me through the word. One time, I remember God giving me the Book of Jeremiah 51:20*:*

"You are My battle-axe and weapons of war: For with you I will break the nation in pieces; With you I will destroy kingdoms."

So, what Jeremiah is telling me here is that I am chosen. Because I've sat down with the Lord to ask questions and inquire what is happening, I feel my people are good and correct and can attend church. They look committed to Christ. I mean, they lived in fear of the Lord. However, it seemed that fear of the Lord was their top priority. What I observed was that people were devoted to attending church every day. How many people attend church daily from 6:00 am to 7:00 am for one hour before work? That's how they begin their day; they're in church every Sunday. But the things I was observing, the afflictions to the people who love the Lord, were not adding up. And after God gave me that verse, I believed that God chose me, maybe to stand as a gatekeeper. Then I remembered I had taken it deeper. I began to cry, asking the Lord what was going on. I don't even understand the reason, and nobody ever can give me the answer to what I am asking for. The Lord directed me to people, completely changing my circle, because He wants to surround you with people who will nurture your God-given destiny. So, my circle changed; I found myself in the company of people who can wage war and pray at midnight, people who are matured, spiritually driven for warfare to unseat Satan from our thrones. This is the kind of people I needed as I warfare. The more I prayed at midnight, the more God began to show me so many things, dreams, and my vision became so clear.

And the Lord told me it's not only what you think people are struggling, afflicted, and suffering with; it's about the foundation. We're going back to four generations. In other words, if you look to today to find answers to the afflictions you see, you may not get the answer because the afflictions are the results of the past generations, sin in the first generation, transgression in the second generation, and inequity in the third generation. That is why God made my eyes open and my ears pay attention to what He was beginning to reveal to me and teach me how to go about it carefully and professionally so that I don't stumble in realms and am not supposed to go to or overstep my jurisdiction and cross boundaries both spiritually and physically.

> **Mathew 5:25:** *"Settle matters quickly with your adversary who is taking you to court. Do it while you are still together on the way, or your adversary may hand you over to the judge, the judge may hand you over to the officer, and you may be thrown into prison.*

God taught me that He is a just judge, so it does not mean when you say, I'm born again, that's all. No, that is a ticket; carry it and take the proper steps to demand what is rightfully yours from the Kingdom of darkness in the name of Jesus. We are talking about how we may have to deal with the sin, transgression, and iniquity of the former generation if no one has taken the right steps of deliverance in your lineage. This means confessing, repenting, renouncing, and asking for cleansing.

Some things are deeper. The Bible says our fathers have eaten sour grapes, and the children's teeth are set on edge. So, even my family, I see now, is the one I'm saying was praying and obeying the Lord, praying from 6:00 am to 7:00 am every day. Those were prayers to sustain them in their daily lives, but nobody researched the cause of negative patterns, cycles, death, etc. And now the Lord spoke to me about the broken foundation: no matter how you try to seal, deny the faulty foundation, it will burst out; the Bible says

Psalms 11:3: If foundations are destroyed, what can a righteous do?

Like Nehemiah, A righteous person must revisit the former, rebuild the broken walls, and remove disorders, bringing them into alignment. Also, the Lord began to teach me, Jeremiah 1:10, to root out, tear down, destroy, overthrow, and then plant and build. So, the Lord started to sort it out for me, piece by piece. Then I seriously began to work with Jeremiah 1:10 and saw some things daily warfare prayer, midnight and fire prayer and realized things were starting to disappear. For example, premature death, limitation, delay, retrogression, spirit spouses, and bondages all those things began to go automatically without even fighting them. I interviewed some of the family members, and they were free from spirit spouses. To me, that was a breakthrough. Some of them don't even know why they no longer see those things, but they're unaware that someone is fighting those battles and making sacrifices behind the scenes. That's why the Bible says *He sent out His word and delivered them all.* That's when one is delivered; God is able to use that person to deliver everyone else. There is true liberation and freedom. The generation is looking for one righteous person to take this assignment seriously and deliver those in need. Some people saw themselves around water bodies, and all that stopped. Some of them were seeing mermaids. They could not see the mermaid anymore.

I began to realize that I was coming from a faulty foundation. A foundation that was faulty before the Lord. I mean, it was not only something to do with the family now; it was going deep. The Lord opened my eyes and showed me what was happening deeper within me up and showed me what was going on deeper into my generation. Things that we don't understand hide deep in the foundation. Now, they are slowly emerging from the depths, coming out of the deep, eating up people with negativity and afflictions. And people will think it is the will of God because they know that if they manifest all at once, you will if they manifest all at once, you're going to discover them and chase them away from you. And that's why I said the prayers our ancestors prayed; they were sustaining people to live their daily lives so that's why I said the prayers our ancestors prayed, they were sustaining people to live on their daily life, but they could not uproot what was planted, which made the root to deepen in our foundation. Once there is a serious born-again person, you begin to see these things and realize there's still more work to do, and are unaware that some have decided to put it on God and say it is the will of God. No, it's not! It is Satan at work.

Otherwise, if you have those people who like those kinds of cold prayers, these things will continue to stay doing what they always do better, which is stealing, killing, and destroying families. The Bible says, 2 Thessalonians 2:7l For the mystery of lawlessness/inequity is already at work; only one is restraining now until he is taken out of the way. God is looking for only that one person who will understand this verse and bring it to work. Since the word is now already completed, what remains is action. And who is to put it into action? It is you and me right now. Each family has that one person. Who is in your family? Will you all continue to be religious, churchgoers, keeping routines and schedules? No, it's time to wake up and fight; arise. The Bible says in Ephesians 5:14, *" Therefore it says, 'Awake, O sleeper, and arise from the dead, and Christ will shine on you.'* Christ is ready to shine on us, but we need to awaken.

When you are still bound by foundational limitations, you can't function fully in your God-given destiny. If one thing needs to excite you to do deliverance, it is that your God-given destiny is waiting for your deliverance to be completed. I can't afford to die without touching my God-given destiny. I will do whatever it takes for my deliverance to be complete so that I can experience what it is like to walk in my God-given destiny.

Proverbs 10:22 The Bible says *the blessing of the Lord makes a person rich and adds no sorrow to it.* So, in the case of my family, as we continually saw premature death burying the young ones, people could boldly say it was the will of God. I can assure you that God was not in it. Where is the will of God? The book of John 1:3 says, *Dear friend, I pray that you may enjoy good health and that all may go well with you even as your soul is getting along well.* Now I ask, why this sickness, infirmity, disease? Why pain, sorrow, why depression? Why schizophrenia? death? Why madness? Is that the will of God? No, the book of Psalms 118:17, *I shall not die but live to declare the good deeds of the Lord.* You need to declare no more death; only the good deeds of the Lord will be spoken in my foundation.

That is how you stop evil. Therefore, you can see that after this point, my foundation contradicted the word in the Bible. That's when I knew, I said, *God, there is more. Please show me what power is functioning on my foundation and what power is commanding my foundation.* What is that strongman and stronghold? There must be a power here that is hidden somewhere! There is a spiritual force that's hiding somewhere. God is unveiling it, uncovering it. In this way, I also realized that my people were just churchgoers, and they were just religious people who were never serious about the things of God. Or they were blind and didn't know if there was more than what they saw and did. For the Bible says, *You shall know the truth, and the truth shall set you free.* So, they didn't know the truth, so they didn't even know they were in cases of bondage; that's how bad it was. The enemy veiled them. But I said, 'God, if you have given me this grace, help me so that I may take this journey to another level; help me rescue my people.'

So, I began to call on the mercies of God; just like Gideon, I looked and saw the things that were going on in my people, my family, and my foundation in terms of sin, iniquity, and transgression. I began to cry, thanking and begging God to have mercy on my foundation. I started to enter more profound repentance, asking God to forgive my forefathers, forgive my ancestors, and forgive Lord, the sin, iniquities, the transgression. I had to go down and enter the new covenant with God because I realized that it is only God's mercy that has kept us until this moment.

In the book of Esther, the Bible says;

> ***Esther 4:16: "Go, gather together all the Jews who are in Susa, and fast on my behalf, and do not eat or drink for three days, night or day; I and my young women will also fast as you do. I will go to the King if I perish, I perish.***

So, I knew that what I was about to start here would not be an easy journey. Esther said, If I perish, I perish." I said, I have to choose between the two. Shall I take the journey, or shall I continue to ride on fake, harmful journeys of my foundation set by the enemies? The Spirit of God told me, *Put on the full armor of God. I'll go with you in the end; surely you will not be a casualty; you will be victorious. God will speak to you in a language that you understand.* So, I put on the whole armor of God, the blood of Jesus, and the weapons of warfare. And then another thing is consistency. Consistency is the greatest weapon of warfare. Also, discipline, then the midnight battle, daily. And then I took the fire prayer very seriously and then fasted. So, let me talk a little bit more about the twenty-three weapons of warfare.

Weapons Of Spiritual Warfare

The first one I'll talk about is the **Missiles of Heaven, the missiles of God** (Ephesians 6:16). The second one is the **Weapon of Blast of Heaven**. Acts 2: 2-28 *When suddenly there came a sound from heaven like the rushing of a violent tempest blast, and it filled the whole house in which they were sitting.* Weapons to blast hemispheres and stratospheres: the galactic realm, the blasting UFO, and the Marine. The hemisphere and stratosphere are supposed to blast the marine spirit by taking control in the name of Jesus over the airways, galaxies, systems, spheres, stratospheres, hemispheres, atmospheres, realms, regions, and domains. Those are the weapons of the blast of Heaven. Another weapon is **God**. And then there's another weapon of **Divine immunity** during the season of influx. We all need to declare divine immunity, and we will be immune to the bacteria and viruses that are meant to kill. Another weapon is **Psalm 7:13**; the weapon mentioned is a deadly one that releases "*flaming arrows*," depicting God as a warrior preparing deadly weapons, specifically arrows set on fire, to use against His enemies. This imagery signifies the destructive power of God's judgment against the wicked. Another weapon is the **Boom of Destruction, the Chariots of Fire, and the Heavenly Algorithm**. The Faraday cage would be used to protect the children of God, like hedging the children of God. No evil can penetrate the Faraday cage. This spire of the Lord is the sword of the Spirit, and another weapon is the **Instrument of indignation** to destroy the whole land.

Isaiah 13:5: They come from a far country, from the end of heaven, even the Lord and the weapons of his indignation, to destroy the whole land.

Also, from the book of Isaiah 13, we have five instruments of indignation; then there's a spear and a battle axe to meet those who pursue us. According to Psalms 35:3, *"Draw out also the spear and stop the way against them that persecute me; say unto my soul, I am thy salvation.* Another weapon when you are in the battle is the **Spear of the Lord, Boom Distracting, Engine of War, Ravenous Bird of the Lord, the Lion of the Tribe of Judah, Chariots of Fire,** and **Arrows of God.** You see, those are weapons. Additionally, we have interception weapons, such as missile interceptors. And then bloom of fire, engine code 2 Chronicles 26:15, referring to machines used to launch rockets from besieged towns. The promo fire Sword of God's deliverance is one of the weapons.

Those are the weapons I wanted to talk about. The weapons that you need in the warfare, midnight prayer battle. The enemy fears nothing but warfare and fire prayer. I have discovered that the enemy didn't understand any other language. The language that the enemy understands is warfare, and the different language that the enemy understands is midnight battle fire prayers. Why am I insisting on this? I've given you an example: I grew up with people I knew could pray, but they were still struggling; they were still swimming between battles, never even getting close to the battle zone. That is why I am confident that it's only warfare that the enemy understands. After doing that, I could tell it didn't take long. I began to receive good reports, even from my foundation. People were coming to Jesus's salvation; revival was breaking through. It was a praise report everywhere, good news after good news. It was like breaking news everywhere; people began to get married, people started graduating, businesses prospered, primary and secondary infertility were wiped away, and people were conceiving triplets. We have seen God. Fear of God entered my people; you could see their commitment to the journey of salvation, carrying the cross of Jesus, was serious. It was like the veil was lifted from the foundation, the family tree. Salvation and revival to many of our members. One thing I realized was that many people were leaving their careers to serve God.

When I hear things happening there, I can only praise the Lord because those are the things I didn't know or believe would come to pass so fast right before my eyes. I thought I was planting a seed for the generation to come. In fact, I thought I was already late to see what I was planting manifest while I was still here. God is faithful indeed.

> *Jeremiah 33:3: Call to me, and I will answer you and will tell you great and hidden things that you have not known.*

I saw the Lord answering the most difficult prayers of barrenness, raising the dead in my family. No one told me anything about God. I saw what commitment to God can do to many things we have already given up.

> *Jeremiah 1:5: Before I formed you in the womb I knew you; Before you were born, I sanctified you; I ordained you a prophet to the nations."*

God is a spirit; for Him to come here and do the work, He needs a pure vessel. I pray that you will be prepared to be used by God. Just speak to Him and say, *Lord, here I am; use me; I surrender all to you.*

Jeremiah 51:20: You are My battle-ax and weapons of war: For with you I will break the nation in pieces; With you I will destroy kingdoms;

People are looking for power in you if you say yes to God's work and serve Him with all your heart. He will give you territories and nations.

Jeremiah 1:10: "See, I have set you this day over nations and kingdoms, to pluck up and to break down, to destroy and to overthrow, to build and to plant

This is where all the attention for deep foundational deliverance is.

Psalms 11:3: If the foundations are destroyed, what can the righteous do?

Yeah, that tells you that God always needs a person who will do something, and then God will use that person as a vessel. But He needs someone to say, "*Here I am, Lord, use me.*" An end-time army to work carefully with God. *This is indeed working.* Chains are broken. Shackles are broken. The cages are broken. Limitations are broken. All because the righteous gave themselves away as a sacrifice to rescue and set free the captives.

In my own case, I see answered prayers for foundational restoration. I see young children graduating with high-flying 4.0 GPAs, which we had lost for a moment, but now good grades are coming home. I see Godly marital settlement, healing, etc. That means we have taken over what the enemy stole and exchanged. Many things have been restored, not only restoration but also with So many things have been restored, not only with restoration but also with compensation.

Psalms 126:1 When the LORD turned again the captivity of Zion, we were like them that dream.

And I thank God for the Deliverance Ministry, because it's clear that God is exposing many things.

After I had performed several deliverances for my own family, the Lord told me I needed to start praying for others. Although this was not part of my life plan, I needed to gain knowledge about deliverance so I can help my suffering family tree. However, it seems that God had a different plan for me. As I began to pray for people online, the power of God was manifesting, and people were being healed and delivered. Just by hearing my voice, even though I am not there physically, people still receive from the Lord. Before, I never knew I could be used as a vessel for someone else's deliverance. It was just a surprise that people could come close to me and fall if they had a spirit in them, or the power of God would overtake them. All this would happen without me saying anything; people will see fire just in my presence or when I speak, and they would begin taking off, running. I was as shocked as the people around me. Firstly, I was not prepared for global visibility.

Secondly, I am a medical doctor, not a pastor, so it is not even in my line of work. Thirdly, all I was suffering for this sacrifice was to remove disorder in my family tree and foundation and introduce order, building a strong foundation in Christ Jesus, which the gates of hell can no longer prevail against forever. So, God did not prepare me either. I am still shocked. How can God use someone like me? I feel like there are so many more qualified people for this assignment than me. Many people are willing to do God's work. For me, this was not the path I chose. All I needed was to learn deliverance to remove disorders in my foundation, and then I could continue with my life. But God had a plan for me.

Some people will come to greet me, and they will fall. If they had any spirits in them, it would manifest. Now, I have begun to understand that God is using me, which is why God is using me: I was ready. I worked on the temple of Jesus Christ, which is my body, a wine skin, so new wine can be poured in, prepared for the work of God ahead. So, God let me work on my deliverance before He could send me to deliver someone else, so that Satan would not accuse me or resist me because of the filthiness of the foundation. God cares about His people. To work in His vineyard requires a high level of purity.

I remember another incident: somebody just came for a visit, and all they could see was the fire surrounding my house. The one who was possessed refused to enter the house and took off because every time I came close to the person, they could only see fire and screamed louder, saying the fire was too much.

In psychiatric hospitals, many mental disorders are spirits and demons just draining taxpayers' money. Because this person was screaming so much, neighbors called the police, and the police could not understand but wanted to take the person to a mental hospital. So, for healthcare workers, please pray over them before you medicate them; it is not a sickness; it is a spirit waiting to be cast out of the body. By the help and authority in the name of Jesus, the spirit was cast out.

Chapter 11:
Understanding the Operation of The Marine Kingdom

The universe is made of three realms: the first is Heaven, then Earth, and then Water. So, marine spirits are marine aquatic spirits that affect people. These spirits originate from water. They are comprised of many spirits in different forms on attack or assignment. It can come from animals like dogs, which may be water and marine spirits. Some of the animals they may encounter in their dreams that could cause attacks are crocodiles, fish, serpents, mermaids, and water nymphs. And there are signs to be aware of if this kingdom is attached to someone. Most of the time, these people dream of finding themselves around bodies of water, in rivers, seawater, ponds, and even the ocean. All kinds of water.

As I mentioned when I began the deep foundation deliverance as a born-again believer, I realized that being born again makes someone a strong man in the spirit. More than before, I was born again, and I discovered many things in my foundation. This is the way I understand it. It's like you are about to learn a new chapter. Being born again is about finding a new chapter, but it falls into two categories: *carnal* and *spiritual*. The Carnal ones still haven't discovered the latest chapter, but the Spiritual ones who have tested the amazing grace. These people want deliverance to reach every child of God because the veil has been lifted, and their eyes can see what others cannot see. Why are *Spiritual* ones serious? Because the Bible says, *I will show you the hidden secrets you know nothing about.* For example, you were being attacked by witchcraft, but as you begin to fight, God reveals all other kingdoms apart from witchcraft that are hiding and quietly waiting to strike at the time of your breakthrough. These are powers of the fathers house which are operating on the altars of Baal that has not been demolished and renounced. So, God, in His mercy, shows you, and you begin to renounce all of them together, and you move on with important things about your God-given destiny after you are delivered from them.

If you haven't dealt with your deliverance, I can assure you that we are sitting between those five kingdoms. Our foundations are faulty because our forefathers didn't know any better. So, if you are not dreaming anything like that, it is just because you haven't touched the actual prayer that will intrude on the satanic camp and begin to demand what's yours. The time you start to demand and do the proper prayer is when you will realize that all this time, your prayers were fanning Satan. The time you are so severely pursuing overtaking and recovering, just like David, is when you begin to see all these things. Some of these things you did not learn from anywhere; they are just personal experiences. You need to be closer to the Holy Spirit so He can teach and direct you as you go.

Certain countries worship marine gods and spirits, and they visit water sites. There are different kinds of marine gods: kings of the sea and queens of rivers. When we discuss marine spirits, we refer to aquatic altars created in the aquatic realm, where sacrifices are offered. We are discussing worshiping marine gods and initiation into their service. Most people were initiated into the marine gods. Our forefathers didn't know any better. Our ancestors didn't know much. That's why the book of Psalms says that some of the sin's I have conceived them in my mother's womb before you even came on earth, so the sin is hunting you and following you unless you cut the cord. Also, in the book of

Deuteronomy, God traces the sin back to four generations, highlighting the importance of confession, renunciation, repentance, and seeking cleansing for one's bloodline.

Some of our fathers took children to wash them and initiate them in the water; that's when the marine spirits took hold of them unconsciously. Now, they are suffering. They took them for protection, and the marine god gave them protection but evacuated all other virtues, every good thing from them, and their life became a struggle until they ran for deliverance. Once you present yourself to satanic territory, you have given Satan one mile, but he will take a million miles from you unconsciously. What Satan needed was an entrance, an open door. Now he did not just come to you, who is seeking him; he has intruded on the entire family tree, bloodline, and foundation unless someone raises and puts a full stop by following the proper steps of deliverance. That is precisely what our fathers did to us, and we are suffering because of their ignorance. But there is amazing grace; thank you, Jesus, for the veil of blindness and ignorance is lifted, and Satan is losing ground once and for all.

As a child of God, you are a burning and a shining light. God has decorated you very well and loaded you with all the beautiful things that Satan doesn't have. If you go to a shrine for help with one thing you need, they give you one thing you want and empty everything else God has given you, "The things you haven't seen yet, those destined to decorate your future, can be emptied by Satan. That's how your destiny becomes vulnerable: it is left exposed, made naked, just by one appearance before a satanic altar or a single seductive sentence.". This is also the same in satanic churches with false prophets who are witches, wizards and warlocks; they do the same thing because they have opened the third eye; they can see through your life and steal everything and empty your destiny. Being careful with your life as a child of God is very important. I pray that you will have the strength to pray and seek the Lord for yourself, rather than running from place to place. It is sad to say that many churches have mixed themselves with Satan; the anointing of God has left. For God is not a God of confusion, and He said Be ye holy as I am holy.

"Satan will take your destiny, your wealth, your glory, and your blessings. Through satanic exchanges, he will place upon your witchcraft, failure, retrogression, sickness, limitation, premature death, divorce, rebellion, disobedience, and addiction. "That is a satanic package. Many of these churches are actually agents of the devil, harvesting souls. Once you're captured into their kingdom, a life of wandering and instability, a vagabond life begins to manifest. You become like a wandering star, without direction or purpose, because you have no control of your life now, your entire destiny is put in their hands, all you are left with is yes, mom, yes sir, some on your knees.

Those who have been initiated in such churches often become stubborn, even toward the Holy Spirit. You can't correct them or give them godly counsel, because their souls are in bondage, they are captives. It will take someone rising up in prayer and spiritual warfare to break their chains and bring them out of captivity.

So that is why it's crucial for every one of us to watch closely our associates and also every child of God, to go through foundational deliverance because no one can escape this. There is not a single family I have seen that doesn't have a mystery of iniquity. The Bible says

> **2 Thessalonian 2:7: For the secret power of lawlessness is already at work; but the one who now**

holds it back will continue to do so till he is taken out of the way.

No one can say I'm good; I have nothing to do with deliverance. Every child of God needs to go through deliverance. We have seen people ignore deliverance; they rise to the top, and the things they have worked for years to achieve crumble in just the blink of an eye. Satan is not to be ignored! That's how wise men begin to think like wise men; Satan is not to be ignored. We don't know what our forefathers did, but our dreams can reveal that something is happening in the family tree, in the bloodline, that hasn't been discovered or addressed. I pray that God will raise a person in your family to find the cause of the mystery of iniquity. You look like you try to live a holy life following the principles of God, but you still experience negativity, cycles, infirmities, and afflictions, all these kinds of things, you live an unfulfilled life which is against the word of God. So that means the foundation is faulty.

What do marine spirits do?

That marine is spiritual. There's a priest, and then there are marine goddesses, who are female. So, goddesses you can also find this (in many perfumes) will usually be female, and goddesses will have a crown. When we are doing deliverance, the Spirit of God will be revealed. Someone has a crown, and once they have that crown, it means they are under the oppression of the Marine Kingdom, and those are the people who never get married and have no spouse; they are dedicated to the water gods. Because that is the crown announcing them, who they are. It doesn't matter what power or what ruler has taken over your life consciously or unconsciously; there is God, He is the final say. Stay in prayer; all these powers will flee. Deliverance through intercessory prayers is good. Because it eliminates everything, it touches the root cause. Don't rush to one-minute deliverance; it's unreal because the church is corrupted today. You don't want to open yourself up for more spirits and demons.

How did we get these?

Much of the information in deliverance ministry we receive from former devil worshipers whom we deliver, once they are set free and receive salvation, they disclose much of the information. Some have an assignment to project and release 150 prostate cancer, breast cancer, accidents, and deaths for sacrifice, per night in territories, neighborhoods of their assignments. The enemy is not resting. We, too, as children of God, are waking up. That is why the bible says while men slept, the enemy came and sowed tares among wheat.

We have a lot of what Satan is doing to the children of God. I don't want to mention certain countries, but they sacrifice their long hair to their gods and goddesses. They will cut their hair, and we see it everywhere. They're having parties, sacrificing to their goddesses after they sacrifice, and now they take their hair and put it in the shop. That's what we buy. We call it human hair. Sometimes, when they are sick or going through turbulence, they cut their hair and take it to the goddesses after sacrificing to their gods, and it ends up in the shops; that is what we buy. It means you purchased goddesses; afflictions, exchange, diseases, you are also being monitored. Also, you buy whatever that person is suffering from and trying to get rid of; that is what you buy with your money. You buy cancer, autoimmune disease, bad luck, and snakes with your money. The Bible says my people are perishing due to a lack of knowledge. I pray that you will not be the one.

So, whoever is using human hair, however, using these artificial kinds of hair, we need to pray so hard for the spirit of discernment because many of these are being sacrificed to the marine goddesses. Marine spirits utilize animals such as crocodiles, snakes, and lizards to operate on the marine altar and afflict people. So, you find people; they have some creatures moving in their bodies. Some of them find live creatures wandering in their environment. Yes, before you call it a pet fire prayer, call on the blood of Jesus and then reverse it back to the sender. So don't take those things lightly. The demonic kingdom is actually at large and is working full-time and overtime to outsmart the children of God and overthrow them. I pray that you will always be awake and discerning in the spirit in the name of Jesus.

So, the Marine Kingdom can also oppress and destroy marriages and families. They plan to breed their marine spirits through human nature, through humankind. So, they come here on Earth and plant their seed. It's like they're on a mission to extinguish humanity. Yeah, they're on a mission to extinguish humanity because when you deliver a lot of people from this marine, and that's precisely what they tell you. If you ask, *What was your job? My job was to sleep with men, seduce men.* They sleep with men, and after they take their semen. They present them to the demonic kingdom, and then what did they say? This is like they mutilated that man; that's why you find so many men are unable to have children. It is satanically manipulated. If you check scientifically, of course, we'll have a lot of answers that will say they have watery sperm or not enough sperm. But according to these demonic Marine goddesses, what did they say? Once they sleep with them, they can never have any children because they know that if there is a legal marriage, a godly marriage, they can keep breeding their children, which will be for the Kingdom of heaven. And their task is to extinguish humanity fully. If they get hold of men's sperm, they take them to the marine lab, and they produce demonic children.

That's why if you have the grace of God on you, not all people working here on earth are people. Some of them are demons. But you need the spirit of God to be able to discover that; just be careful, for they have a special assignment, too. They are not here to joke; they have a special assignment. So, they destroy marriage, they destroy families, and they fire arrows of sickness, infirmity, and disease from that kingdom to the children of God, which means there's an exchange of health that is in the children of God. That's why we have so much premature death.

These days, it's even worse. Someone will wake up, and if you have a little pain, when they go to the doctor, the diagnosis will be stage 4 uterine cancer. You are dying. They have traded in their long life; they took your life to elongate their own. A person they put cancer on so that they can die satanically and prematurely. I pray that it will not be your portion as a child of God. So, the only way to be able to escape when the doctor is giving you the diagnosis, you have to say immediately right there, *That's not me. I reverse back to the sender*. Don't say, *Yes, I agree*. You know, that's an exchange from the Satanic Kingdom. The next time you go to check, that stage four breast cancer will be gone. So, we need to raise soldiers who understand that many things are unreal, fake, satanically projected; even the doctors were surprised you were their patient. They did regular checkups all the time, and suddenly, stage four breast cancer. That is what it is: marine kingdom assignments. By the grace of God, we are also coming to a vicious end; we are no longer tolerating this nonsense in the name of Jesus. If you see people with womb issues all the time, they have miscarriages, abortions, bleeding uterus all the time, missed menstruation, barrenness, and all these things are because their womb has been submitted to the marine kingdom and has been used by the satanic kingdom. Yes, they know if you are going to have children, those children will serve the Lord, and so their assignment is to stop that breeding of a clean generation as soon as they can and introduce their evil agenda. Also, when they cause miscarriage, it could be that they are using that womb for their sacrifice. which is a clean sacrifice for the pregnancy is sinless.

So, when you pray with understanding, you receive deliverance. Your womb will be open, and you will receive children in the name of Jesus. Your womb will be protected from satanic manipulation. We have had so many people like that; the marine kingdom is the one that causes it.

Marine Kingdom agents' agenda is to spot shining stars, rising stars, glory, and blessings, and ensure they find a way to get around that person and evacuate everything possible. When they succeed, they must replace what they have exchanged with something else. Their replacement is always the opposite; it is evil. exchange thrones, evil coverings, family chaos, and the downfall of ministries. So, be careful who is around you. Remember, Satan will always be there, and you may not know him because he is clothed in sheep's clothing. One thing I can tell you is the Bible says bad company corrupts good morals, so please, if you are around satanic friends, they are always looking for what they can steal or exchange from you. The Bible says, do not be ignorant of the devices of the craft. The Bible says only prayers will push the Kingdom of darkness away. I pray that you will keep your fire-burning altar burning in the name of Jesus Christ.

Sex is another weapon the marine kingdom uses as a weapon, both physical sex and spiritual sex, for those who have not been delivered from spiritual spouses, the demon who does sex in the dream. All that is to make sure they get fluids from you and take it to their marine altar, and your family can never see the full glory of God once they have your property, like semen, body fluids, nails, hair, cloth, certificates, etc. Unless you fight them hard through prayers, making them uncomfortable in your body and dwelling. Also, I will send angels of God to locate your properties wherever they are in the satanic kingdom and retrieve them back to you. Through sex by a physical satanic agent, they can access the family; for example, if they get a married man or a married woman, they automatically get access to the children. They begin to empty the destinies of young children. That's how they start to manipulate young children. If you are unaware of the spiritual realm, you will start to fight children, not knowing it is the spirit at work. Some of these spirit spouses have been part of the entire family clan; that's why you often find them already interacting with young children in dreams. I have had so many parents present cases like those; as a medical doctor, they will think it is a disease for a child to be sleeping but having sex loudly in a dream like real sex. Until God opens up their spiritual understanding, these parents will begin to fight on their knees, not in doctors' offices or hospitals.

> *Ephesians 6:12: "For we do not wrestle against flesh and blood, but against the rulers, against the authorities, against the cosmic powers over this present darkness, against the spiritual forces of evil in the heavenly places.*

Many of these spiritual powers, personalities, and demons have had access to our lives because many of us took prayer casually. My way of saying this is, if you give Satan a mile in your life, he trespasses and goes a hundred miles. That's the truth. A woman confessed that once they get hold of a man's physical sex, that is the beginning of the downfall of that entire family, and their life can never be recovered again unless by the mercies of God. "Remember, Satan is already in the church. That good-looking man could be a satanic agent, and that good-looking lady could also be a satanic agent. They know the church is a gathering place for innocent people but please, do not be ignorant, the world is dark already."

Another weapon the marine kingdom uses is money; once they get hold of your money, the money you have given with good intentions, they place it on their altars and take your real money, leaving you struggling with finances. Those are just a few examples we have received from real-life people on assignments that we have had the opportunity to pray over and deliver them from the kingdom of darkness; praise the Living Jesus.

A satanic agent confessed that another weapon they use is sex. They plant a monitoring spirit in your body. They put a spiritual ring before sex. When they enter womanhood, they leave there, and their assignment is to monitor your entire movement for twenty-four hours through their satanic satellite. Satan is not playing; they are ordering your steps once you are under their satellite. Yet, the Bible says the Lord orders the righteous man's steps. I pray that the Lord may not find any unrighteousness in you, and may the Lord reveal to your things that you need to agree on and repent so that the accuser of the brethren will not find any ground to accuse you. Remember, Satan can never intrude on you without a legal right. Satan is the best advocate; he knows all the laws physically and spiritually. So, don't be in denial; put down your ranks, education, wealth, and fame and run to God for cleansing and purity. You need God, and God needs you, but you have to be pure to escape Satan and rest in the hands of the Lord God Almighty, for He says, *Be ye holy as I am holy.* In *Zechariah 3:3-5,* **Joshua, the high priest, stands before the father, and Satan stands to accuse him because Joshua, the high priest, was dressed in a filthy garment.**

Marine Kingdom can access you through perfumes. Many perfumes are considered demonic, especially those from certain brands. If you read the contents, you will see things like Medusa, the demon with many snakes on the head, or goddesses, the god of water. So that is what you are putting on, and that is what you are attracting: satanic angels. Marine clothes with snake skin: You wear snake skin all day and keep snakes in your house. Those spiritual snakes are choking your life, constricting your life, and ordering your day. You cannot be delivered from the snake kingdom if you still have snake material in your closets. You have snakes on your perfume and shoes. Observe the gifting, like candles. Many scented candles are scented with spirits. If you are spiritually active and awake on the day they bring these candles into your house, you will encounter severe battles in dreams, finding yourself in strange meetings with people or wandering in forests, etc. Please pray carefully about everything.

Again, human hair is also a marine product filled with spirits, and some of this hair they get from people as they die, so that death will be hunting you; in other words, you have accepted their sacrifice; it is just a matter of time, whether by disease or accident. Please stay prayed on; my people are perishing due to a lack of knowledge. Artificial nails, most of the fake stuff, all are from the marine kingdom; that will make a person change from what God created them to be like. I pray that your eyes will open, and you will seriously begin to care for yourself. So, these kinds of people are hard to correct. I beg pastors to be patient because you know it is not, they disobeying, but the spirit they are wearing is the one in charge of that body.

Additionally, you can acquire marine spirits by sharing items, such as clothes. Also, through sacrificed food, they sacrifice their food to their god first, then call people to eat or give them free food. Be careful of the celebrities who have not given their lives to Jesus. Most of their gifts have a spirit attached to them. Watch and pray. Do not be ignorant of the devices of the craft. If you are still not serious about your God, Satan is already serious. Remember, there is a battle in the spirit, and the rule is simple: the higher power will always win. So, my question is? Is your God still powerful, or is it just a name? Are you born again and love Jesus? That's it? Is the vessel that is holding God still pure or not? Is the word of God active in your life? How about your prayer life? That's how you are going to overpower every other god. The Bible says, *Hebrews 4:12* **For the word of God is alive and active. Sharper than any double-edged sword, it penetrates even to dividing soul and spirit, joints and marrow; it judges the thoughts and attitudes of the heart.**

And that is how the lesser power bows. In many restaurants, they sacrifice food to their god. Be sure to take authority and take charge everywhere you go, including territories, cities, airports, restaurants, and meeting areas. Take charge and take authority. Satan likes gathering, so at every gathering, just know there are satanic agents, too, who have an assignment to steal, kill, and destroy. So, be mindful to take authority as a soldier of God by claiming it in the name of Jesus. By doing that, you are rescuing many children of God who are still ignorant of the spiritual realm. Life is so spiritual. Ask God to trim your circle, and be careful who you allow in your inner circle. If it is a ministry, you still need people; anything in this world, you still need people, but let God lead and send them; He is so faithful, and he will do that.

Another weapon they use is to astral project in your life. Remember to pray daily to cut the silver cord of astral projection from any satanic kingdom; that's our daily prayer point. Cut every silver cord of astral projection from any kingdom in the name of Jesus. Whatever is projected against you children, spouse, career, business, destiny, health, your thrones, ministry, marriage, or family will automatically fail and be reversed back to the sender. Remember to shut down all the time in the 1st and 2nd heaven in the mighty name of Jesus and disrupt their communication system. Scatter their satellites and mirrors, and command their transportation system to disperse into irretrievable pieces by the authority in Jesus' name. You always have to interfere and interrupt their work. Don't just sit and pray nice, nice prayers. Satan understands contention and violence; that's why the Bible says in Mathew 11:12 *From the days of John the Baptist until now the kingdom of heaven has suffered violence, and the violent take it by force.*

Ninety-nine-point nine (99.9%) percent of the born-again Christians I have met are still praying in the name of Jesus, but praying nice prayers. I pray that God will open your eyes to see what surrounds your family, community, and territory. Until the veil is lifted and you begin to see in the spirit the next minute, you will join the company of warriors and pray like a mad prophet.

Ancestral covenant can cause marine Kingdom to have legal rights on you

Our fathers worshipped a god in the rivers, in the water, and what you need to do is confess, renounce, repent and ask for cleansing; that's how we remove the legal rights.

How do you fall prey to the marine Kingdom?

It could be through your mother or your father. When your biological parents are submitting to this god, or pregnant women exposing their pregnancy, and young babies who still can't defend themselves are vulnerable. Please mothers, hide your pregnancy and babies physically and spiritual, pray for them.

One can also fall prey to marine attacks through satanic music, which is enchanting and releases spells. Their instruments, rhythm, and rituals, like their evil finger signs when dancing, are to collect souls. Some can even go deeper and use highly influential satanic agents where they gather so many people at once and cause a stampede where there will be human sacrifice and blood sacrifice to appease their gods without question. Spiritually blind people will think it is an accident; no, behind it, there is a spirit. May God help us to be open to learning, for the world is moving at a speed that many of us are not yet ready for.

Another way someone can fall prey to marine spirits is through consulting occult powers, through false prophets and false churches, and visiting shrines and satanic altars. You are a child of God, and you love Jesus, but you are submitting to a demonic kingdom agent who is your pastor.

Please keep your Bible closer and read your Bible so that you will know when the manipulation starts; you can run for your soul. How do you spot false churches and run for your soul before it is too late? One, they are prideful; they exalt themselves and take pleasure in receiving glory. They are more of a fame, prosperity, sin, no repentance, no conviction, no rebuke for sin and evil, fornication, manipulating scripture to favor and cover up their evil, sleeping with and impregnating multiple women, and commanding abortion so they can sacrifice to their gods, also sacrificing people yearly, especially those that are closer to them. By accident or by disease, someone must die because their evil covenant is demanding its part of their covenants. The major assignment they have is to harvest souls for hell. If your pastor is one of these things, please don't worry about how many miracles they can perform or how much wealth they have from water spirits, because God Yahweh is not in it, choose God and run for your soul before it is too late.

Don't be fooled, for the Bible says, 1 Peter 1:16, *that as God is holy, believers should strive to live a holy life, mirroring his character and purity*; essentially, it's a call to live morally and ethically as God does. Please, the word of God is final; I don't need an explanation. If it's not aligned to the word of God, get out as soon as you can; run for your soul and enlighten others by rescuing one more soul. The focus should be on Jesus alone, on the blood of Jesus alone, not on the man of God, not on anointing oil, not on handkerchiefs, not on anointing water. Stop running from one place to another looking for a solution; you'll fall prey before you know it. Seek God; He is faithful; He will speak to you through His word. God has been talking to you, but you are occupied with so many things you can't even hear the whispering voice of God. I pray for the spirit of the

Mighty to rest upon you and begin to pursue the Lord with all you might.

Be careful with tattoos; many of them hide marine spirits. Not fashion, remember Satan is craft, so don't be ignorant. Some hide satanic power in those tattoos to direct their prophecy and power, so it looks real.

Also, be careful with the many handkerchiefs they use. When they touch your forehead with those handkerchiefs, they may be swapping your destiny and star, and opening your third eye—connecting you directly to their gods.

> *2 Corinthians 2:11:* **So *that Satan will not outsmart us. For we are familiar with his evil schemes.* This is the word of God.**

What are the signs that you are under Marine spirits?

Number one is dressing up in seductive clothing, which I feel sorry for men, and this is not only for unmarried women but also for those who are married. I feel sorry for men, and I pray that God will hide their eyes so the surroundings will not tempt them, but will focus on Jesus. The second sign that you are under marine spirits is exposing your body parts, breasts, and thighs, and they don't care. Why? Because it's not people; it's a spirit behind in control. The third sign that you are under marine control is having uncontrollable sexual urges. After this pastor touched me, some people have said that's where their problem started. So, those are some examples of pastors who are agents of the marine kingdom. They touch you; they impart to you that with the marine sex demon, you are always in need of sex. Another sign you are under marine spirits is opening a satanic shrine in your house for sex, for example, masturbation, pornography, or sex toys. As you do that, all the spirits know they can come to your home anytime and invite even more spirits. In short, you are inviting a battle you cannot fight.

First, it is difficult to chase these things away even when you are done with them because you made them a home, a portal, and an altar. Until you close that portal, open a godly portal, and be serious with God, they can leave you alone again. Another sign that you are under marine spirits is failure at the edge of breakthrough, constant sex in dreams, lust spirits seeing dogs in dreams, swimming in water and walking in water bodies in dreams, seeing marine animals, snakes, crocodiles, and alligators, and consistent hardship, no matter how you try; unexpected losses of finances and properties; you are under marine oppression and monitoring. Other signs are failing relationships, extreme poverty, and financial crisis. Another sign that you are under marine control is being gifted items in dreams, such as jewelry, chains, and rings.

How do you overcome and destroy marine spirits?

Confess, renounce, repent and ask for cleansing. Begin to live a life that honors the Lord; fear of the Lord is the beginning of wisdom. Maintain purity, holiness, and righteousness. And then get rid of satanic possession and satanic representation in your house. I have told people to clean their closets because you cannot chase a marine spirit out of you while you have so many things in your home that represent the aquatic kingdom. Activating warfare prayer and fire prayer, read the word of God, commit yourself fully to the Lord, and serve the Lord. Start self-deliverance slowly. Self-deliverance does a perfect job; self-deliverance is indeed Jeremiah 1:10, for it is carefully done. When you do self-deliverance, you are sure that no root can remain untouched.

Chapter 12:
What Is Your Birth Right and What Is False Birth Right

Generational Birthright

And this is what the Spirit of God revealed to me: most of us live a false generational birthright, and many don't even realize it. I was praying during the Midnight Battle when the Spirit of God opened my eyes. I saw this writing: "*Somebody is living a false generational birthright.*" I spoke it out loud. Then, the Spirit of God ministered to me: according to Psalms 51, the sin, iniquity, and transgression we inherit from our mothers' wombs still follow us, with the legal right to remain attached to us. The Bible says, "***Behold, I was brought forth in iniquity, and in sin my mother conceived me***" (Psalm 51:5). This iniquity has been passed down through generations: what my mother found in her womb, her mother saw in hers, and so on. It is a transgenerational mystery of iniquity; the chain is long, and it continues as long as no one breaks it. It's the same case when you visit the doctor's office for a check-up. They will ask you about any diseases that run in your family. These are generational afflictions, and they should be taken seriously. One needs to begin rejecting them, denying them access through confession, renouncing, repenting, and seeking generational cleansing.

> *Jeremiah 1:10: "See, I have set you this day over nations and kingdoms, to pluck up and to break down, to destroy and to overthrow, to build and to plant.*"

This is why it's so crucial for someone to rise and stop this nonsense. It's my prayer that this book will awaken many. We need someone to rise and say "*No*" to these generational curses. Your generational birthright from God is aligned with the faith of our forefathers Abraham, Isaac, and Jacob. We are the seed of Abraham, the root of Jesse, and the sons and daughters of Mary. What is being referred to here is a blessing passed down from one generation to the next. But today's generation is living in contradiction. We have become vulnerable to negative patterns and cycles passed down through the generations. Few are willing to research and understand what happened and what can be done to break free from this cycle. Instead, many simplify it by saying it's the will of God. No, it's not, inequity belongs to Satan.

Your Generational Birthright Was Swapped Who Swapped It?

The Lord showed me that many are living a false generational birthright, but one can stop it if you choose to do so through confession, repentance, renunciation, and asking for cleansing from the Lord by His mercy. The right we have is not the generational birthright, according to Father Abraham, but according to Satan. Why? Because our past generations submitted to Satan, and they not only submit themselves but also sold out the entire family tree, the bloodline, and even future generations. This is wickedness on another level. That is why you can trace alcoholism, addiction, premature death, and other destructive behaviors from one generation to the next, yet you still blame the children. No! If the foundations are destroyed, what can the righteous do? (Psalm 11:3) They sold out even the unborn generation. They sold out good health, wealth, thrones, shining stars and intelligence. They sold their daughters to spirits. Now, this generation is living in confusion and an unsolvable mystery!

> *2 Thessalonians 2:7: "For the mystery of iniquity is already at work. Only he who now restrains it will do so until he is taken out of the way."*

Who is the evil man or woman in your family tree or bloodline? Who is the satanic agent in your lineage? I pray that you will raise the bar of prayer higher than your contemporaries in your family tree until that hidden satanic agent is exposed.

On the deliverance ground, spirits manifest in people. I once encountered a young lady who walked like an old woman. When I asked her why, she replied, "*I am her grandmother, my spirit lives in this lady. I hindered her progress because her destiny was sold out, and now no destiny is left for her.*" Another young lady manifested like a man. When asked why, she responded, "*I live here to ensure she remains un-submissive to her husband, or her marriage will not endure. Why? Because we have compromised the destinies of all the women in this family, transforming them into uselessness.*" "We have taken their uterus; we are using them for monthly blood sacrifices. We have cut their menstruation short (here, Doctors will tell you it's premature menopausal) to support their scientific argument. They will also say we have shut their wombs, and they will be barren. (Doctors will say it is infertility." God is against what Satan is doing to the children of God. God is answering His name, and He is against all satanic lies.

These issues come from the foundation, but God, in His mercy, reveals these things to us in spiritual knowledge and understanding. It is up to us to pay attention and begin to recover the damage Satan has caused to our foundation. The

Bible states that *Jesus came to destroy the works of the enemy* (1 John 3:8), and the time is now. So, when you see struggles in Christian family's pain upon pain, unanswered questions that cause doubt and condemnation, you may be living a fake birthright. There is a twisting of the foundation, a manipulation and exchange of your destiny. It has nothing to do with you.

I pray for you in the name of Jesus. By the authority in Jesus' name, anyone sitting on a generational fake birthright, I reverse it in the name of Jesus. Whoever has done this, may the Lord locate and rebuke them in the name of Jesus. I bind these generations to the spirit of the living God and declare that from today, only the birthright of Father Abraham will be effective in these generations in the name of Jesus. I take authority in Jesus' name and shut every satanic portal that has been opened to the fake generational birthright. I open a godly portal to this generation and restore the original birthright now in the name of Jesus.

When the Devil Has Requested to Torment Your Life

The Holy Spirit led me to discuss two types of "*born again*" believers: those who are just born again and those who understand the rights of a believer as a child of God.

1. **Just Born Again**: These individuals love the Lord and seek security, assurance, and insurance in Christ. They want to hide under the name of the Lord so that if they die, they can enter heaven. However, here on Earth, they don't strive much. They are in their comfort zone. These people tend to give up on confronting the devil and instead accept whatever comes their way, even attributing misfortune to the will of God. For example, if a baby dies or a pregnant woman passes away with her baby, they might say, "*It's the will of God.*" These believers can't enjoy life

on earth because they don't pursue repentance, renunciation, and cleansing to regain their original right. As a result, their rights as believers are limited due to legal covenants working against them. This kind of generation is in bondage and will remain in bondage forever while in Christ Jesus.

2. **Born Again Who Understand Their Rights**: These believers are like lions and lionesses in the spirit. They have studied spiritual truths and know that life is spiritual, and they must fight to receive what God has already promised them. They are persistent and determined to pursue, overtake, and recover all. The Holy Spirit leads them to see the light and understand that they are not just born again for heaven but to bring revival to those around them, to break bondages, to turn generation pages, and rewrite family history.

The question is, why did the Holy Spirit choose you to be a serious born-again? The answer is simple: you are the one who has seen the light, and the Bible says, "*The light shines in the darkness, and the darkness has not overcome it*" (John 1:5). Your purpose is to shine in the darkness and bring light to those around you, especially those who are "*just born again*" saying every evil happening is the will of God. "They have neither the courage nor the strength to take authority, to unseat the enemy, and to dislodge him and his evil loads out of the way. You, on the other hand, carry the scepter of truth and battle to war without compromising. In Isaiah 47:1, Go down, sit in the dust, Virgin Daughter Babylon; sit on the ground without a throne, queen city of the Babylonians. No more will you be called tender or delicate. It is time someone arises and unseats the virgin daughters of Babylon, for there is no more throne for them.

"Consequences of Rising as a Believer

Once you rise as a believer who understands your rights, you become a threat to the enemy, especially your foundation. The enemy, knowing that you are a threat, will look to attack you either spiritually or physically because you are disrupting the satanic operations in your family and community.

Many consequences come with being a serious believer. The enemy may seek to destroy your foundation, but as you press forward, you must remember that you are never alone in this battle. The Bible says in James 4:7, *"Submit yourselves to God. Resist the devil, and he will flee from you."*

As you engage in spiritual warfare, especially at midnight, you must present the blood of Jesus and the power of the cross and confront the enemy. This is where the power is, and you must take authority over every evil operation against your family and foundation. God is watching, and He will strengthen you to overcome; in the end victory is guaranteed.

Chapter 13:
Testimony Midnight Battle

Anyone who has succeeded in engaging in a midnight battle has a story to tell. They will tell you, "*I broke free after I became disciplined and consistent at midnight*." When I say midnight prayers now, I mean you join a company of warriors who fight together. The Bible says, "*Iron sharpens iron.*" If you don't have the strength for midnight prayers alone, join a group of saints who do. I believe many pray at midnight, so find one.

At midnight, we come as soldiers, as an army, to chase a thousand. Deuteronomy 32:30 says, "***One can chase a thousand, and two can chase ten thousand.***" So, you come strong and expectant, knowing that you are backed by God in the name of Jesus Christ of Nazareth. During midnight prayer, you come with understanding, knowing that every time you're there, at least one or two things are being uprooted from your foundation. I don't care how many years they've been planted there. If you remain consistent and available for this midnight battle, foundational evil is uprooted daily.

Another thing you need to pray for is the grace of God to help you remain consistent in this battle. Remember, "*pray without ceasing*" (1 Thessalonians 5:17). The enemy can influence your daily schedule if you let him, and before you know it, you may find yourself with no time for God. When I was "just a believer," I often gave excuses for not praying: *"I'm busy," "I'm working, "I have children," "I have a husband," "My schedule is full,"* or *"I just don't have time."*

171

But God is jealous of us. One day, I heard a whispering voice say: *"Am I not the one who gave you all of this? Did I make a mistake in blessing you? I need you. Turn to me, and I will show you how to manage all of this and still have time for me. Remember, I am your number one priority. "Revelation 4:1* After this, I looked, and there before me was a door standing open in heaven. And the voice I had first heard speaking to me like a trumpet said, "Come up here, and I will show you what must take place after this." If you let God lead, you will not be frustrated.

But then I heard a preacher say, *"Any excuse you give to avoid prayer is to your disadvantage. Now I knew that I was on the disadvantaged side because my life was busy."* I realized that everything you do in the Kingdom of God is for your benefit. Nothing goes unnoticed by God, and He rewards those who diligently seek Him. So, I stopped giving excuses. I realized the enemy used my busy schedule to keep me from praying, so his evil roots can continue deepening. But I also knew that God's calendar would always set time aside for me to pray and deny me peace until I obeyed.

I also know some believers who simply say, "Pray for me," or send a prayer request. While this is good, for a prayer to be truly powerful, it needs agreement. You may be sick or going through life's challenges, but I encourage you to find strength and be present at the prayer altar, whether through Zoom or in person. Be there, and agree with other saints.

The Bible says, *"One can chase a thousand, but two can chase ten thousand."* Don't be the person who sends a prayer request and then goes to sleep. When you are present and in agreement, it gives legal spiritual access to the person praying for you to enter your family territory and begin to uproot any satanic plantations or manipulations affecting you and your household. In other words, you need to be aware of what is being done on your behalf. Also, God needs your direct attention and not from the other person. That is a commitment to your Father.

This is why prayer must become our new normal. Pray in the airport, in the office, in the kitchen, anywhere. This is what it means to pray all the time. Practice praying in tongues, but don't confuse "*praying all the time*" with "*Midnight Battle*." The enemy does not give up easily. Remember, you are a first-generation commander. What you are doing, no one in your bloodline has ever done before. The enemy has been riding on your blessings, glory, and family's wealth unconfronted, unchallenged, and unopposed. But now, you are the first to say, "*I'm taking back what the enemy has stolen!*"

The Bible says, "**You shall know the truth, and the truth shall set you free**" (John 8:32). Because you now know the truth, you are armed to confront the enemy. The Bible also says that **when the thief is caught, he must return seven times what he has stolen** (Proverbs 6:31). So, you come in the name of Jesus, claiming what belongs to you.

The enemy will attempt to intensify his attacks on you, employing heavy weapons to deter you. However, remember that this battle is not yours. The Bible says, "**He who sits in heaven shall laugh**" (Psalm 2:4). God has already won the battle, and victory belongs to you because the battle belongs to Jesus.

The enemy may intensify his attacks, but your job is to resist him. "**Submit to God, resist the devil, and he will flee from you**" (James 4:7). You have to resist him repeatedly, don't stop. The more you resist, the weaker the enemy becomes. Our weapons of warfare are never exhausted because the source of our power is God Himself, and He will never run out of strength.

During midnight prayer, you must wear the whole armor of God. The astral projections of the enemy will target your weakest points, but when you are vigilant and pray, you dismantle their schemes. They will use high-tech equipment to monitor and afflict you, but your prayers can destroy their operations. These attacks can manifest as physical ailments but are only distractions from the enemy's true agenda.

You must remember that when engaging in spiritual warfare, the enemy is constantly seeking opportunities to attack. The enemy will use astral projection to afflict you with sickness, poverty, rejection, confusion, and other forms of bondage. But God is watching, and He will not let the enemy win. The enemy may try to cause discord in your relationships, but you must stay steadfast in your prayers. When you resist him, you are reversing everything he's trying to do.

Victory belongs to you, but it requires consistent discipline, persistent prayer. Don't let the enemy intimidate you. When the enemy tries to afflict you, whether through physical pain, confusion, or temptation, don't just accept it. Reverse it seven times stronger in the name of Jesus. And remember: the key to effective warfare is repentance. Without repentance, there's a wall between you and God. But when you repent and forgive, you remove the legal rights the enemy has over you.

So, during midnight prayers, be vigilant. Consistency is key. Keep your altar strong and active, burning with fire. The enemy fears persistent prayer because it destroys his works. Stay in the battle. Keep fighting. Remember that every midnight prayer you engage in is breaking down strongholds, uprooting evil, and preparing the ground for God's victory in your life.

Chapter 14:
Your Money, Your Fertility, Your Star, And Your Spiritual Destiny

Guarding Your Star and Spiritual Protection

In the Book of Matthew, Chapter 2:11-12, it says,

"When they saw the star, they rejoiced with exceedingly great joy. And when they came into the house, they saw the young child with Mary, His mother, and fell and worshipped Him. Then they opened their treasures and presented gifts to Him: gold, frankincense, and myrrh. And being warned of God in a dream that they should not return to Herod, they departed into their own country another way."

Your star is shining and can be seen by two kinds of agents: demonic wise men or heavenly wise men. Therefore, you must always pray that your star will be in good hands. The Spirit of God has led me to speak and warn parents, fathers, and mothers about this important matter.

In today's world, many people are obsessed with social media. When a woman conceives, she often shares the news on social media. But please understand this: Satanic agents are everywhere, and they are constantly looking for a mother and her baby. Do not expose your young children to social media until they are old enough to understand the risks and defend themselves. I understand the excitement and the joy of sharing, but there are wolves out there. As a parent, it is your responsibility to protect your children, both spiritually and physically.

You are carrying a pregnancy to protect the baby inside your womb, not to expose the child to all kinds of negative influences in this world. You may think you're only sharing your joy, but unknowingly, you could open doors to spiritual dangers. You are hurting the child by exposing them prematurely to the world's negativity.

How do you protect the child during pregnancy? Through prayer, declarations, commands, and renunciations for the unborn child. Remember, we are doing this based on Jeremiah 1:10: to uproot and break legal covenants. A legal covenant can still have power over your life as long as it exists. That means there is still access to these opposing forces working against you. This is why you see negativity pass from one generation to the next. Satanic agents can retrieve everything before the child is born because you have exposed the child to the world. They are selling your child's blessings before the child enters the world.

If you haven't dealt with the foundations of your life and the generational patterns in place, your pregnancy might be under attack. If you haven't broken these patterns, Satan can easily steal from you—by remote control because the doors are still open. It's easy for him to get what he wants from you. If you haven't dealt with your foundational issues through Jeremiah 1:10, you are vulnerable to satanic arrows, and they are trading your soul on the satanic market.

It is essential to take control of your spiritual realm because whoever controls the spiritual realm controls the physical realm. Your spiritual authority determines how your day goes, what happens, and what you allow and disallow. You may wonder why everything seems to fall apart despite hard work, why you struggle to break through and keep losing. That's because the covenants in your bloodline are still active. Psalm 51:5 tells us that we were conceived in sin, and these generational curses chase us.

That's why I urge you to examine the spiritual foundation you're building before you conceive. Identify any covenants in place, declare, confess, renounce, and ask for cleansing for your child. Command the breaking of any negative patterns that may have followed you. Pray that your child will not fall into the traps that have ensnared past generations. Take authority in Jesus' name and proclaim that no evil can touch your child, the fruit of your womb. Speak life into that child, commanding that they will not fall victim to the same cycles of sickness, autism, disease, or developmental delays. You are the gatekeeper for your children.

When pregnant, praying continually, especially during the midnight hours, is crucial to break any negative foundational strongholds. You must be vigilant in warfare prayer before, during, and after childbirth. Even after the baby is born, continue to pray and protect them, for the enemy is always watching for an opportunity to strike. Pray for their future, including their spouses, and declare that no evil will come near them. You are praying to secure their future and prevent them from falling into generational traps. You must do this as parents because God has entrusted you with His seed.

> **Proverbs 22:** *"Train up a child in the way he should go; and when he is old, he will not depart from it."* If all parents understood this and took their responsibility seriously, many future problems plaguing our children would be avoided.

What is happening in your life results from your star not being properly guarded. Your star may have been tormented, stolen, or captured. It may have been divided and scattered, leaving you with an empty star. When the enemy captures your star, so is your soul. That's why many people don't understand the struggles they face—both their soul and their star are under captivity.

That's why you must pray that your soul will escape from the snare of the fowler and that your star will be released. Command your star to come out of captivity and locate you. Pray for the restoration of everything that has been taken. When the enemy controls your star, they control your life.

On the day of delivery, prayer is essential. Pray that the first person who receives your child is a wise man, not a demonic midwife or doctor who seeks to steal the child's star. Some medical professionals are agents of darkness. Even if you cannot control who is there, continue to pray that no evil force will have access to your baby.

Financial Protection: The Power of Tithing

Another critical area to address is money. As children of God, we are meant to operate in heavenly currency. Since you have already begun working on your foundation through deep deliverance, continue praying and stand firm in the truth of God's word.

Philippians 4:19 says, "***And my God will supply all your needs according to His riches in glory in Christ Jesus.***" However, many children of God are not experiencing the abundance promised by this verse. Why? Because there is a devourer in place. The covenants of disobedience speak against prosperity.

One major cause of financial scarcity is disobedience to tithing. In Malachi 3:10, the Bible commands us to bring the full tithe into the storehouse. God says, "***Test me in this, and see if I will not throw open the floodgates of heaven and pour out so much blessing that there will not be room enough to store it.***"

The devourer thrives in disobedience. If you are not tithing, you allow the enemy to operate in your finances. As a child of God, I encourage you to tithe faithfully and watch how God will bless you in ways you never imagined. Remember everything you put in the hands of God; he will multiply it. He will not give you back the same as you gave to Him. This is financial security. Jesus had only five loaves and two fish to feed the multitudes. He lifted them up, He thanked God, and gave the multitude. Five thousand men ate, we don't know how many women and children there were. But what we know God multiplied what Jesus presented to Him.

When you give your tithe, no matter how small it may seem, present it to God with a heart of obedience. Pray it will speak for you, prospering your hands and work. Once the devourer is dealt with, you will see the glory of God manifest in your life. You will experience prosperity, unexpected increases, and the fulfillment of God's promises, for the hand of the Lord is on your finances.

Obedience in tithing leads to financial security because you are sowing seeds for the future. Disobedience, however, allows the enemy to steal, kill, and destroy. The spirit of destruction and confusion will plague your finances if you fail to obey God's commands.

I struggled with tithing at first. I thought 10% of my income was too much to give, but the Spirit of God told me it wasn't about the amount. It's about obedience. God trusts me to manage what He has given me, and when I show Him that I can be faithful with a little, He will entrust me with much more.

So, as you walk in obedience, know that God will open the floodgates of heaven. Your prosperity will flow, and no evil will come near your finances. You will not work for money, but money will work for you. I pray that you will recover generational wealth and that God will raise up a generation that fears and obeys His word, securing their legacy in His kingdom.

To survive in this dark world as a believer, you need to keep the Book of the Law with you. Let God's word lead and guide you. He has promised to provide for you and bless you abundantly, but your obedience opens the door to His blessings. I pray that you will receive wisdom, understanding, and the courage to obey God in every area of your life, including tithing.

OBEDIENCE

The world we live in is a dark place. I advise you to keep your Bible handy and follow only what God has instructed you to do.

> *Malachi 3:10: "Bring the whole tithe into the storehouse, that there may be food in my house. Test me in this," says the LORD Almighty, "and see if I will not throw open the floodgates of heaven and pour out so much blessing that there will not be room enough to store it."*

Disobedience is the greatest enemy of God and the enemy of your destiny. If you want your destiny to align with God's plan, pray for obedience. Obedience to the Lord brings the fear of the Lord, which leads to wisdom. Through wisdom, you will grow closer to God, experience His glory, attract angels, receive blessings, and be disciplined in the things of God. It will also help you stay consistent in your faith and actions. Obedience will drive Satan away from your life and bring alignment, restoration, healing, deliverance, prosperity, and continuous income streams through heavenly currency. In this life, everything you are looking for is clothed in obedience.

FERTILITY

The Bible says in Isaiah 34:16, "*Look in the scroll of the LORD and read: None of these will be missing, not one will lack her mate. For it is His mouth that has given the order, and His Spirit will gather them together.*"

This scripture assures us that God is in the business of family. He acknowledges holy families and desires for families to flourish.

> *Genesis 1:28: God blessed them and said, "Be fruitful and increase in number; fill the earth and subdue it. Rule over the fish in the sea, the birds in the sky, and over every living creature that moves on the ground."*

God has already given us direction. Our lives are like a script that has been written, and all we need to do is follow it. For every child of God, our lives should align with the Word of God. If anything in your life does not align with God's will, you have the right to question it. Many of us have questions today, so we find ourselves in deliverance ministries, seeking answers about our past mistakes and learning how to live a life free from satanic manipulation and contention. We also seek guidance on how to improve the future for future generations.

Today, fertility has become a significant issue, and the enemy is at work behind many manipulations. Satan's agenda is to destroy God's pure seed and corrupt the human body. Infertility, in many cases, is a result of satanic manipulation. In married couples, many experience:

1. **Ovulation disorders:** Problems with the release of an egg from the ovary.
2. **Endometriosis:** A condition where tissue like the lining of the uterus grows outside the uterus.
3. **Uterine abnormalities:** Such as fibroids, polyps, or an abnormal shape.
4. **Tubal damage:** Blockage or damage to the fallopian tubes.
5. **Sperm problems:** Low sperm count, poor sperm quality, or problems with sperm movement.
6. **Hormonal imbalances:** Issues with thyroid, estrogen, or progesterone.
7. **Lifestyle factors:** Smoking, excessive alcohol consumption, obesity, or being underweight.
8. **Age:** Fertility declines with age, especially in women over 35.
9. **Genetic factors:** In some cases, infertility may be caused by genetic mutations.
10. **Unexplained infertility:** In about 25% of cases, no identifiable cause is found.

All these are factors that affect the reproductive system that disqualify one to carry and host a baby from zero to nine months.

Unexplained infertility is particularly concerning. When your understanding opens and you turn to God, these issues can be overcome without spending money. Couples can still receive their blessings, but must turn to God for intervention.

Why is Satan working so hard to stop your seed? It is because your seed is a holy one, carrying a bloodline that has the potential to break generational curses and change the course of history. Satan knows that if this child is born, it will destroy his kingdom on earth. Therefore, he will do everything in his power to prevent your womb from being fruitful. He will send you to doctors who will give you reasons why you should struggle with having a baby or never have one at all. This is when you must recognize that the enemy is at work and begin to confront him through prayer, fasting, renouncing, repentance, and seeking cleansing to close any legal doors the enemy may have opened through your foundation, territory, or lifestyle.

Psalm 11:3: "If the foundations are destroyed, what can the righteous do?"

BATTLE OF THE SEED OF THE WOMB

If the foundations are not dealt with, the womb that has been shut might open through prayers, but without addressing the legal steps, the result can be miscarriage, stillbirth, or birth defects, even death. If the baby survives these challenges, the battle continues into the neonatal period, sometimes leading to sudden infant death syndrome (SIDS) or even the mother accidentally smothering the baby while sleeping.

If the child survives these battles, they may face struggles in adolescence, such as addiction to alcohol, drugs, turning children into devil worshipers, or gender confusion. This cycle will continue unless the underlying foundations are addressed. If the foundation is destroyed, what can the righteous do? The battle for the womb is not just physical; it is spiritual. The righteous must rise and rebuild the broken foundation.

Satan does not attack without a legal covenant in place. There is a reason why certain battles continue in families. As long as the door remains open, Satan will continue to destroy things. This is why prayer is so important. Pray without ceasing. Men ought to always pray, for it is through prayer that we can push Satan out of the way.

It is easy to surrender to God, renew your covenant with Him, and ask Him to start afresh with you, repenting for the sins, transgressions, and inequities of past generations. When you make a bold covenant with God, He will bring blessings and restoration where there seems to be none, He will remove disorders that follow a faulty foundation. The Bible says, "*You may not see the rain, but your valley shall be full of water.*"

Satan has already tried to take over the unborn generations due to our ignorance and carelessness, but now we must confront these battles in prayer and seek deliverance. Every "*why*" you ask creates a more significant battle, for the enemy becomes furious. But you must stand firm in faith and prayer, knowing that you are above them, seated in heavenly places with Christ Jesus at the right hand of our Father, far above powers of darkness, Principalities, and satanic rulers of this world.

HOW SATAN SHUTS FERTILITY

From a medical perspective, men sometimes face challenges where their manhood is attacked, making it difficult for them to father children. This could be through conditions like erectile dysfunction (ED) or azoospermia (lack of sperm). Many men will struggle despite counseling and medical treatment. But the Bible says, "*Submit yourself fully to God; resist the devil, and he will flee from you.*"

I have seen God restore what seemed impossible, strengthening individuals once again and granting them the blessings of children. Satan also attacks men through lust and spirit spouses, creating friction in marriages and making them feel disconnected from their spouses. These attacks can lead to separation or divorce if you are not vigilant.

Women's reproductive organs are often attacked as well. Some women may experience premature menopause or hormonal imbalances that cause their menstruation to stop. But I have seen God's power move in miraculous ways, bringing back menstruation and fertility where doctors have no explanation. Satan thrives on ignorance, but those who understand the spiritual realm can confront these issues in the name of Jesus Christ.

The Bible says, "*He has given us power to trample on serpents and scorpions and all kinds of powers of darkness; nothing by any means shall harm us.*" When we confront Satan, we do not do so in our own strength but in the mighty name of Jesus Christ. We go armed with the blood of Jesus, the power of God, and the understanding of who we are in Christ Jesus.

Satanic manipulation is real, but when we confront it with God's power, we break the chains and restore what the enemy has stolen. Whether through spiritual warfare or seeking medical intervention, we must remain vigilant and trust in God's ultimate power to restore us to health and fertility.

Uterus and Spiritual Warfare

The way spiritual attacks on the uterus occur is through the sending of spirit spouses, also known as demons of sex, in a dream. These spirits ensure they have intercourse with individuals, often manifesting in dreams. They are responsible for causing issues like fibroids. There are various types of fibroids, and I've seen many cases, especially in women. I recall one surgery where the fibroid was as large as a nine-month pregnancy. Upon opening the womb, it wasn't just one fibroid but multiple, all growing together like potatoes on the branch of a tree. I'm referring to this kind of fibroid, where the uterus, intended to nurture a baby, is instead filled with fibroids. These are tricks of the enemy.

Some fibroids, particularly intramural ones, are so deeply embedded in the uterus that even after surgery, they cause significant damage. These fibroids require deep removal, sometimes from the innermost layers of the uterus. This can lead to complications that prevent the uterus from carrying a child, even after healing. These are satanic manipulations of the reproductive system designed to prevent women from bringing forth life. But our God is faithful. Such situations require deep and detailed deliverance. There are also cases where adhesions form, causing layers of the uterus to bind together and occupy the space meant for the baby. In such cases, doctors may inform women that they may never have children. But let me declare that God can give children to women without a womb or those in menopause. Our God is not to be underestimated.

Other severe attacks from the enemy can be ovarian cancer, uterine cancer, and cervical cancer. These are part of the battle for the womb. Women, arise and pray before the enemy advances. The enemy seeks to prevent you from fulfilling your God-given purpose, and doctors may even reach a point where they suggest removing specific organs like the uterus. All this ensures that your womb does not bring forth a seed.

I have interceded for many women, and by God's mercy, I have seen miraculous turnarounds. God prepared me not just as a medical doctor but also to confront the enemy and declare, "*This is a lie.*" These attacks are real. I have seen them with my own eyes. I have operated on women whose fallopian tubes were deliberately cut to prevent them from conceiving. Some of these women have been left with only one fallopian tube or one ovary. However, I have witnessed God's miracles whether they had one or none. I have seen women who were deemed unable to have children, even those without a womb, carry babies from zero to nine months. This is the mighty God we serve. These kinds of miracles leave scientists and the world in awe. There is nothing God cannot do. You have not yet seen the extent of what God is about to do for His children. He is still on the throne, rules, and works miracles.

The Bible says, "*You are the God of all flesh; is there anything too hard for You?*" (Jeremiah 32:27). This is the God I am talking about. I have seen His miracles with my own eyes. So, fear not, child of God. Submit yourself fully and resist the devil; he will flee from you (James 4:7).

In John 8:32, the Bible says, "*You shall know the truth, and the truth shall set you free.*" Only the truth will help you claim your rightful destiny, as mentioned in Jeremiah 1:10. Until reality sinks in, it is impossible to tackle the spiritual battles. If you don't confront these spiritual battles, you will not experience the fruitful destiny God has for you. You are called to give birth to a new generation, to rewrite your family's history, and to establish a clean bloodline.

The enemy will try to prevent you from fulfilling your purpose, but God says otherwise. As a medical doctor, I have come to realize that spiritual battles are far more challenging than any medical challenge. I used to neglect the spiritual realm, dismissing its power. But the more I resisted God's work, the more I became confused, even though I was a child of God. I faced real battles—difficulties in conceiving, multiple miscarriages, and threats to the health of my pregnancies. It wasn't until God opened my eyes that I began to see the true nature of the spiritual realm.

That was when I understood that I had been neglecting the most important battle of all—the spiritual one. I began to take my spiritual life seriously and realized how vital it was to align with God's will and to take authority over the enemy. We must fight with knowledge, and we must pray strategically to secure our spiritual destiny.

Spiritual Destiny and Warfare

As children of God, our destinies are filled with blessings, glory, and health. Satan, knowing this, works tirelessly to intercept these blessings before we even realize they exist. The enemy can see the potential of our spiritual destiny long before we do. That is why they work relentlessly to steal it from us even before birth. These blessings are precious to the enemy because they are marketable in the Satanic realm, where they can be sold or used for their own purposes.

Many afflictions—autism, cerebral palsy, Down Syndrome, gender confusion, and other developmental disorders—are increasing because they are rooted in spiritual manipulation. Medical diagnoses often disguise these afflictions, but behind them are spiritual forces working to sabotage God's plan for people's lives. Some doctors are beginning to realize that these issues are spiritual in nature and are turning to God for help.

We must pray and stand firm in our faith to recover our spiritual destiny. Persistent prayer, especially during the midnight hour, can help us break free from the enemy's grip. Midnight prayer is powerful because it disrupts the enemy's work, and we can recover everything the enemy has stolen. The enemy hates those who are persistent in prayer, especially during this time, as it interferes with their office and plans.

We must also pray for our families and bloodlines. This is not only about us but also about the generations to come. We have to protect our spiritual destinies, our families, and our children with God's protection, and we must do so consistently. Satan wants us to live carelessly, but we must wake up to the reality of spiritual warfare.

A person's spiritual destiny can be left vulnerable through ignorance or neglect. This is known as a "*naked destiny*," especially for children who can be easily stolen. However, we can cover our destiny and the destinies of those around us through prayer and spiritual vigilance.

The Bible says in John 10:10, "*The thief comes only to steal and kill and destroy; I have come that they may have life and have it to the full.*" We must protect our spiritual destinies, understanding that the battle is spiritual and that the enemy can only steal what we fail to guard.

With knowledge and understanding, we can engage in warfare and reclaim what the enemy has stolen. We must arm ourselves with the whole armor of God (Ephesians 6:10-18) and speak the Word of God with authority, knowing that the battle belongs to the Lord. When we do this, we become vessels God uses, paralyzing the enemy's powers and destroying their works.

In the issue of fertility, if the root cause is a faulty foundation, women may face repeated miscarriages or infertility. These issues can be the result of blood-sucking demons or demonic altars in the family's bloodline. These demonic spirits feed off the blood of family members, requiring sacrifices to maintain their power. Such attacks require intense spiritual warfare, and families need to confront and dismantle these altars through prayer and deliverance.

Chapter 15:
Raising the Standard of Prayers

Raising a Standard of Prayer That Puts the Devil to Flight

When we aim to raise the standard of prayer, we must consider all kinds of prayer, not just one. The Spirit of God will guide you in knowing which type of prayer to engage in, depending on the situation. That's why having the Word of God in you is essential, as God speaks through His Word. A prayer led by the Holy Spirit is the prayer that brings breakthroughs and answers.

First, you must receive salvation. The Bible says in 2 Corinthians 5:17, *"If anyone is in Christ, he is a new creation."* Salvation is essential because it grants us access to the deep things of our Lord Jesus Christ.

Second, repentance is crucial. Repentance separates us from sin and evil, not only on a personal but also on a generational level. Just as Gideon did, we must trace our ancestry back, repent for the sins of our forefathers, and cry out for mercy. Psalm 51 provides a powerful example of repentance, as David laments the sins and iniquities of his ancestors. This prayer is a cry for mercy for our generation, bloodline, and family tree.

Additionally, forgiveness is key. The enemy can use unforgiveness to hinder your breakthroughs. That's why it's important to forgive, not hold grudges, and ensure your heart is free. Without forgiveness, it becomes harder to enter a prayer of mercy, as seen in Gideon, who sought God's mercy after discovering the idols his ancestors had worshipped.

Our forefathers may have done things that have caused spiritual battles, afflictions, and challenges in our lives. These generational issues require us to cry out for mercy. The Bible says, "*The mercies of the Lord are new every morning.*" God renews us daily, regardless of our foundation, but we must raise the prayer point, acknowledging the sins and iniquities in our lineage.

Some foundational covenants are deep, and you need God's help to tackle them. I once delivered a person, and the spirit said, "*We've been here too long. Who are you to come and take us down?*" When I asked how long they had been there, they responded, "*Before Christ.*" Sometimes, demons lie, but sometimes, they tell the truth. If a demon has been in a family for over 2000 years, no one has ever confronted it. It's time to say, "*Enough is enough,*" and seek the Lord for wisdom and deliverance.

This is your time. No one else will, if you don't rise up to confront these afflictions. Your ancestors may have asked the same question: "*Is there anyone who will stand up?*" God is here to help, and we can pray a prayer of mercy. A mercy prayer never fails.

Next, we enter a warfare prayer. The Bible says, "*Pray without ceasing*" and "*Pray in tongues.*" If you haven't received the gift of the Spirit, may you be baptized in the holy ghost in the name of Jesus. Pray in tongues at home, at work, in the car—everywhere. Before you know it, you'll pray for hours.

Midnight prayer is a powerful weapon. Pray between 12 a.m. and 4 a.m. This is the "*midnight battle,*" when the enemy is most active. By praying at midnight, you confront the enemy before they can act against you. The enemy fears confrontation, and as long as you remain passive, they will continue to thrive in your territory. But if you confront them, they must flee.

When you pray at midnight, you take authority, decreeing that the enemy will not succeed against you. You are interrupting their plans and nullifying their attacks with the blood of Jesus. You are in their camp, declaring that they will not make any decisions against you tonight. You are engaging in spiritual warfare, sending back all the satanic arrows directed at you and your family. You are blocking the enemy from advancing.

As you do this, you invoke Hebrews 12:29, which says, *"Our God is a consuming fire."* By the authority of Jesus, release the fire of God against the enemy's plans and the altars they have set up against you and your family. Everything they plan to afflict you with is nullified and neutralized by the blood of Jesus.

Consecration is also essential. You must live a fasted life, seeking a deeper encounter with the Lord. During fasting, remember that *"this kind can only come out by prayer and fasting"* (Mark 9:29). It's during these fasts that God uproots and tears down strongholds, as described in Jeremiah 1:10. You must stay in a place of prayer, consecration, and fasting to break deep spiritual battles.

> *Jeremiah 33:3: "Call to Me, and I will answer you, and show you great and mighty things which you do not know."*

Sometimes, the deep things of our foundations require us to go deeper in prayer and fasting. After fasting and seeking God through His Word, you will receive revelation and insight into the deep things that must be dealt with.

God will reveal these generational issues through deep fasting. Through this process, God trusts you as a generational commander to break these chains. The Word of God is your spiritual food, and as you feed on it daily, your spirit comes alive, and you walk in the supernatural.

To walk in the supernatural, you must be disciplined and consistent. We are consistent in worldly matters, but we often lack discipline when it comes to spiritual things, the things of God. Consistency and discipline are crucial in God's work. When you are consistent, you gain access to God's secrets, which lead to breakthroughs.

In raising the standard of prayer, remember that Daniel prayed in the upper room, facing Jerusalem. This act signifies accessing the deep things of God, a place of higher spiritual authority. To access the deep things of God, you must go higher. In prayer, fasting, and giving, you must go deeper. The deeper you go, the greater your victory.

Acts 1-2 reveal that the disciples were instructed to remain in Jerusalem until they received the power of the Holy Spirit. They waited in unity, and when they were in one accord, they received the baptism of the Holy Spirit. This is the power you need to raise the standard of prayer that puts the enemy to flight.

Prayer can be done alone, but it's powerful to pray with others. The Bible says, "*One can chase a thousand, and two can chase ten thousand*" (Deuteronomy 32:30). God's power is released in unity. As it says in Jeremiah 9:17-21, women gathered to mourn and pray for the restoration of their city. Prayer in unity is powerful; when you pray together, God releases His fire, power, and angels.

Find someone to pray with. Whether it's your family, a prayer group, or a friend, praying together in unity is crucial. As seen in Acts 2:1-4, when the disciples prayed in one accord, they received the Holy Spirit and were empowered to fulfill their mission. A special grace and anointing are released when we come together in prayer. Don't go through deliverance alone; find a group, join in unity, and be fully connected to receive the full power of God.

PRAYING AT MIDNIGHT: THE OFFICE OF THE MIDNIGHT

This is the office of the Midnight. From 12:00 am to 4:00 am, Midnight Prayer can unlock more spiritual breakthroughs than any other prayer time. Here are five reasons why you should start praying at midnight:

1. **Midnight prayer is a time for divine encounters**, where chains are broken, and doors are opened.
2. **Midnight prayer is a battlefield of the spirit**; more spiritual attacks and destiny exchanges happen at midnight.
3. **Midnight prayer is the hour of deliverance**, the time for divine judgment to be activated against the enemy.
4. **Midnight prayer is a time for divine favor and open heavens**, where God releases favor and blessings.
5. **Midnight prayer answers why Jesus prayed at midnight.** In Luke 6:12, Jesus went to the mountain and prayed all night long.

If you are still sleeping and expect a great destiny, I sound a trumpet to you, Child of God. Wake up from sleep, wake up from slumber—let's pray! This reminds you that you will never recover from the enemy until you add more strength to your prayers and engage in the midnight battle.

The purpose of rising at this hour is to confront the enemy. It is to declare that we are no longer in fear, and we know what the enemy has done to our forefathers because they slept and slumbered at midnight. This generation has found the truth. We are bold, and we rise for the midnight battle with understanding. We are consistent in our pursuit to overtake and recover all in the name of Jesus. The bible says While men slept, the enemy came and sowed tares among wheat.

This is a tired generation that seeks the truth to be set free, the generation of *"Enough is enough."* This is the generation of John the Baptist. The Bible says, "***From the days of John the Baptist until now, the Kingdom of God has suffered violence, and the violent take it by force.***" The John the Baptist generation is already here. We also carry the scepter, the Sword of Jehu, to bring down the Babylonian kings and ensure that the entire house of Ahab is demolished. No Athaliah will remain in our families, foundations, or territories of assignment. We know who we are in Christ, so we take authority in the name of Jesus and reclaim the thrones and crowns that our forefathers gave up to the enemy ignorantly.

It's time to command the virgin daughters of Babylon to step down from the throne and sit in the dust. There is no throne left for them. At midnight, we are returning our thrones of foundation, birthrights, legal inheritance from our fathers, and blessings from Abraham, Isaac, and Jacob—the thrones of good health (3 John 2) and prosperity and alignment to the will of God.

> ***3 John 2: Beloved, I pray that in every way you may succeed and prosper and be in good health, just as your soul prospers.***

The enemy captured all our thrones, and we are living a life inconsistent with the Word and promises of God. Ecclesiastes 10:7 says, "***I have seen slaves on horseback,*** *while princes walk on foot like slaves.*" All these things happened while men slept. The Bible says, "While they slept, the enemy came and sowed tares." We are awake; we will no longer sleep or slumber. We are a recovering generation on the battlefield.

In other words, we are telling the enemy this will not come easily. We are ready to fight, but we are assured that we will never be casualties at the end of this battle. We are guaranteed victory because the Bible promises that the battle is not ours; the battle belongs to Jesus. We take control, dominion, and authority in the midnight battle. Midnight is not for everyone; it is for those who have already understood their purpose in prayer, for those who have been trained in other prayer times. When you can manage the midnight battle, you have graduated from other prayer times, and spiritually, your rank increases. You know that something has shifted in the spirit.

Midnight is for soldiers, like Jehu, Esther, Deborah, and others, ready to execute God's tasks here on earth. Midnight is for those who carry the generational scepter and are prepared to open the scroll and read it. We come in the volume of what is written about us and our families. The midnight battle is for those saying, "*I will see this assignment through from start to finish. As we recover from this battle, I want to see results, fruits, and positive family changes.*"

When you engage in midnight prayer, you declare that you will not be one of those sleeping while the enemy is stealing. You tell the enemy, "*No, you will not succeed anymore.*" This battle ends with you. It will not be passed on to the next generation. The midnight battle is all about confrontation. You tell the principalities and powers, "*There is a new principality from the Kingdom of Heaven. Get out of the way."*

In **Exodus**, when God sent plagues to Egypt, He distinguished between the Egyptians and the Israelites. When He released the swarms of flies, they affected only the Egyptians, not the Israelites. So, at midnight, you rise and declare, "*No fly zone.*" You can fly anywhere but not in my zone.

When you pray at midnight, you are equipped with spiritual weapons missiles from heaven, arrows of fire, chariots of fire, etc. Psalm 144:1 says, "***Blessed be the Lord, my strength, who teaches my hands to war and my fingers to fight.***" When you clap your hands in prayer, you terrify the kingdom of darkness, interrupting their work. You nullify their assignments with the power of Yahweh.

You come with thunder, fire, and lightning in the midnight battle. Revelation 16:18 says, "***And there were flashes of lightning, rumblings, peals of thunder, and a great earthquake such as there had never been since man was on the earth.***" You call for earthquakes, seaquakes, and spiritual turbulence to disrupt the enemy's plans. You also call on angels to support you, as this is a battle.

When you pray at midnight, you ascend in the spirit, and your spiritual position shifts. You shut the first and second heavens, disrupt the enemy's communication systems, and dismantle their altars and shrines. You command their sacrifices to dry up by consuming fire. You arrest and restrain their agents, cutting the silver cords of astral projection, and command angels of blindness to blind all monitoring spirits.

If the enemy dares to touch you, they will die by correction. Victory in the midnight battle comes through discipline and consistency. If you do this daily, no enemy can stand against you.

You can reverse their evil works by sending them back seven times stronger. The enemy also has ways to reverse your prayers, but you must come against the spirit of backlash, retaliation, and repercussion, by the enemy. Seal every prayer point with the blood of Jesus and put on the whole armor of God to remain impenetrable by satanic weapons.

> *Isaiah 54:17 "No weapon formed against you shall prosper, and every tongue that rises against you in judgment you shall condemn."* The enemy will not surrender easily. They will continue firing arrows and cursing you, but you declare that their curses will not prosper. You build a wall of fire around your life and your assignments.

As you engage in midnight prayer, the enemy will begin to leave you alone. Kingdoms that have held you captive the Marine Kingdom, Water Spirit Kingdom, Serpentine Kingdom, Witchcraft Kingdom, Animal Kingdom, and spirit spouses will lose their power over you. Evil dreams, such as those involving dead relatives or witchcraft, will stop. Your dreams will be replaced by divine dreams, and victory will be yours.

Congratulations on the victory ahead. Keep fighting the good fight!

Chapter 16:
The Prayer of Repentance Forgiveness from Your Ancestral

Look at Psalm 51, and let's consider the case of Gideon. In Judges Chapter 6, when Gideon was chosen, the first thing he did was come clean with God. He said, "*Look, my tribe is the least, and I am the smallest in my family. Not only is my tribe the least in Israel, but I am the least in my family.*" In other words, *out of all the tribes, all the people Lord, didn't You find anyone else to use except me?* That's when God tells Gideon he is a mighty man of valor. This shows that God looks deeper into one's heart than outward circumstances.

This brings us to an important point: God is looking for one person in every family, clan, foundation, generation, and bloodline. He knows He may not be able to find everyone, but He is searching for at least one person. That person is someone He can use to transform their family, bloodline, or generation from darkness to light. It's someone who can bring light into the darkness.

God will isolate the chosen individual and teach them great things secrets of the Kingdom until they are ready for the assignment. In the deliverance ministry, it is always the case that whoever is ready is chosen. You cannot simply be ready. When you feel a deep prompt or burden to go into deliverance, it means the time for your family and generation to be delivered has come. God has been focusing on you, and He has chosen you. Those ideas are not your own; it is the mind of God speaking to you, urging you to rise, put on the whole armor of God, and go to work to deliver the people God intends to reach through you.

Looking at Judges Chapter 6, verses 15-18, we see Gideon's response in verse 15: ***"Please, my Lord,"* Gideon replied, *"How can I save Israel? Indeed, my clan is the weakest in Manasseh, and I am the youngest in my father's house."*** This tells us that Gideon was not ready and neither are we. We are not prepared until we feel the kind of force, the type of power that confronts everything denying us rest, peace, and sleep. You may feel it: something must be done, and when you look around, you see that no one else will do it except you.

If you are reading this book or listening to this message, you are the one. It's not by accident. God is speaking to you, telling you the time has come. He has found you worthy, and He has chosen you to bring light into your life—and through you, into the lives of others.

FOUNDATION

The topic of repentance and forgiveness for the sins, iniquities, and transgressions of our forefathers and ancestors is a profound one. The reason is that when you trace back what our ancestors or forefathers did to the Lord, you'll see that some of these things may hit you. For example, there are stories where, when a king died, he had to be buried with 12 live young virgin girls. This is just one example. Or an elder who could not pay a debt because of his authority over the clan had to sell all the future generations to spirits, meaning they would never qualify for physical marriages. Or he might sell all the males in the clan to wandering star spirits or vagabond spirits. These are just a few examples. So, if you're wondering what's happening with your children, their lives are deeply spiritual.

Such things cannot go unpunished, even though someone might say, "*Oh, I have received Jesus, and everything is fine.*" We must reach a point of agreement. Until their last breath under the sand in the grave, those souls were crying before the Lord. Even now, they are still crying. The Bible says that the blood of Abel continually cried to the Lord. There is blood crying out, and that blood needs to be comforted.

> **Matthew 5:25**: "*Settle matters quickly with your adversary who is taking you to court. Do it while you are still together on the way, or your adversary may hand you over to the judge, and the judge may hand you over to the officer, and you may be thrown into prison.*"

Remember that this verse is in the New Testament, after Jesus. This brings us to the conclusion that God is and will always be a just judge. Satan is familiar with the laws and legal rights. That is why, through our carelessness and failure to pay attention to the details of the word of God, Satan accuses us every single time. Christ and His blood, His death, help us navigate this by confession, repentance, renunciation, and asking for forgiveness. You cannot simply close your eyes and say, "*I received Jesus; everything is okay.*" No, it's not okay, until you, who has seen light, stand and follow the correct protocols and procedures of the Kingdom of our God to demand your foundation to be transformed from the Kingdom of darkness to the Kingdom of light. That is how you are going to see a relief in our families, community, and nation.

This is where we see Gideon. When he went to tear down the altars, he found all the gods his ancestors had built. What happened to Gideon? He began to feel overwhelmed and immediately saw the filthy, stinking idols in the territory of his fathers. He said, "*What my forefathers have done, I don't even know how to please God. What can I do to please God?*" At that moment, Gideon sought peace from God. He said, "*If I can only attain peace with God, I'll be fine.*" But after seeing the state of his ancestors' sins, he realized it was dirty and sinful. This is when Gideon's eyes are opened, and he recognizes that he came from a faulty foundation. Before this moment, Gideon was unaware. Many of us are unaware of the foundations we come from, so it's safer to avoid self-righteousness. Don't count yourself wealthy because you don't know what your forefathers did.

Immediately after, Gideon built an altar, calling it the "*altar of peace with God.*" Gideon understood that he first needed to ensure he and God had settled the matter. God then told Gideon, "*Go, peace be with you.*"

So, we, too, need to find a place. If you are chosen, you will need to find a place to sit, talk to God, and cry out to Him. The way I did mine was through Psalm 51. This chapter is fulfilling for repentance. It starts by saying, "***Have mercy on me, O God, according to Your steadfast love, according to Your abundant mercy; blot out my transgressions, blot them out, wash me thoroughly from my iniquity, and cleanse me from my sins.***" And you see, this verse says, "***For I know my transgressions, and my sins are ever before me.***" They are ever before me until I renounce them and come into peace with God. Unless the sins, iniquity, and transgressions are no longer there, they will always be before me.

Let's look at verse 4: "***Against You, You only, have I sinned and done what is evil in Your sight.***" And you may be justified in Your words and blameless in Your judgment. Now, I want you to pay attention to verse 5, where he says, "***Behold, I was brought forth in iniquity.***" In other words, I had no part in what I was going through, but I was brought into it. "*And in sin did my mother conceive me.*" Even my mother's womb was filled with sin. How did that sin settle in my mother's womb? It means that my mother, too, was sitting in sin in her mother's womb. And my grandmother, from her mother, and so on. So, as you trace this sin, you can tell it's a continuous covenant.

Until God speaks to you, you may not realize that it will follow everyone, including your children and grandchildren, if you don't stand boldly to break this chain. It will be there until you come to this understanding and break it. In verse 9, David says, "*Hide Your face from my sins and blot out all my iniquity.*" In verse 11, he says, "*Cast me not away from Your presence and take not Your Holy Spirit from me.*"

This tells us that God can turn away from us because of our sins. The Bible says God speaks once, speaks twice, and if you don't perceive it, He will turn away. If you hear God saying, "*Hey, start your deliverance,*" and you stay silent, that means He's turning away. That's why David says, "*Do not turn away from me because of my sins.*" According to this verse, I can tell you that God has turned away from many of us after we received salvation, because we thought that salvation meant the work was done. But salvation is to bring light into the darkness of your foundation, to deliver your people.

Are you surprised that many are born again, love the Lord, attend church, but still face unspeakable troubles? Salvation means you put on Christ Jesus and go to deliver God's people, bringing healing and restoration to those still in satanic bondage. Darkness cannot deliver darkness. How can you receive salvation and remain comfortable in your zone while seeing children wasted from the womb, in their youth, teens, and even as young adults? The enemy goes deeper to cause untimely death and premature death, and you're just watching.

I understand you didn't know what to do before. But now, rise, put on the whole armor of God, and let's go to midnight together to learn as the Spirit of God teaches us through prayer. Let's end some of these evil things once and for all. We can still make this world a better place.

God is waiting for us to act and break those evil covenants. Many of us, however, don't want to delve deeper and put in the hard work. Everyone wants to plant and build, but where are you building? Are you building on a faulty foundation? While the base of your foundation might seem reasonable, the root is still shaky. That's why when you get serious with Jesus, that's when the war begins. You disturb the faulty foundation. If you haven't confessed, renounced, or repented, according to the enemy, you're still one of them, even though you've received Jesus. That's why they can still access you and trouble you however they want.

The Bible says, "*If the foundations are destroyed, what can the righteous do?*" The righteous will not just say, "*Jesus finished it all.*" They will take the necessary steps to rebuild the faulty and broken foundation in Jesus' name.

The Bible tells us about the foolish men who built their houses on the sand, and when the wind blew, their houses were destroyed. This is us when we want an easy build. No one wants to uproot the root first. But no matter how much you ignore the root, it will continue to grow and spread wider.

We don't want to delve into the foundation before we build on it, which should be the rock. A foundation built on the rock will not be moved, and the gates of hell cannot prevail. If you see the gates of hell prevailing in your life, there's something in the foundation that hasn't been dealt with. There's something the foundation is crying out for, waiting for someone to settle the matter. But you're busy closing your eyes, worshipping, and going back and forth to church while troubles and trials multiply. You are busy moving from one false prophet to the other seeking deliverance. You may change churches, but no one else will deal with your foundation if you don't address this matter now.

If you hear this message and have thought about deliverance but remain silent, it's waiting for you. Perhaps you have more grace to delve deeper into your bloodline's full foundation of deliverance. Don't keep dodging it. It will remain until someone steps forward to address it.

When will you decide to go deeper and take care of the foundation? Let's look at Deuteronomy 5:9: "*Thou shalt not bow down thyself unto them, nor serve them, for I the Lord thy God am a jealous God, visiting the iniquity of the fathers upon the children, unto the third and fourth generation of them that hate me.*"

So, you are standing on the foundation of people who hate God. Let me repeat it: you are functioning from the foundation of people who hate God. You may trace the sin of your past back to four generations, but even in your generation right now, some may still be continuing the sins of your forefathers, still visiting demonic altars. If they are connected to you by bloodline, even though you are born again, you must work very hard.

As long as you are still connected to people who have not been born again and continue those sinful practices, they may still ruin your salvation journey.

When they go to their altar, they may try to take you down because you are a child of God. If you stay in God's presence, God will speak to you, and you will work to take them down. And this is because your power is more significant, you will win.

So, not only the sins of the past four generations but also those still connected to you may be getting God angry. If you have people like this, your journey of deliverance will be the most challenging because they will closely monitor and scrutinize every step you take. You'll feel like you're taking one step forward but ten steps backward because there are powers against you.

Now, you must rise, be bold, and stay consistent in prayer, especially at midnight prayer. Communicate with God, and He will continue to give you secrets. You must stay close to God and never avoid midnight. Many are ignorant of this, starting deliverance but taking it casually. You must be diligent; don't sleep after you've launched the battle. Otherwise, the enemy will counterattack and overthrow you.

Those who understand this don't joke. No joke. No excuses. Forward we go, upward we go; no turning back.

Now, coming to the point of being connected to people, this is why you need to be angry in the spirit and align yourself with God. That's how God will help you, and through Him, you can nullify the power of those people. When you consecrate yourself, cleanse yourself, confess, renounce, and repent, God can help you straighten your foundation and that of your family. If you live according to the ways of the Lord, pleasing Him, God sees your heart. Since you are connected to this family, this generation, this bloodline, you are like the one who sees the light and will bring that light to everyone around you. While they are in darkness, your light will shine and overshadow theirs.

Eventually, they will have no choice but to surrender their false gods and return to the one true God.

For those who are stubborn, persistently using their gods' power to try to bring you down, they will be taken down, just like in Daniel Chapter 6. There, those who plotted against Daniel and put him in the lion's den ultimately failed. Daniel came out alive. Our God is a mighty man of war, a Lion of Judah. He is not a God to be taken lightly. The word of God promises us that we will never be casualties. We must never be casual. In the end, there is victory, but we must first submit to the Lord.

James 4:7 tells us, "**Submit yourselves, then, to God. Resist the devil, and he will flee from you.**" Deliverance requires practical submission to the Lord. You can't resist the devil in your power. Without submitting to the Lord, victory is impossible. Submit to Him, live by His laws, and please God in all you do. Live a prayerful life, read the Word of God, be Spirit-filled, and learn to hear God's voice. That's how you become a friend to God. Many say they are for God but are not truly friends with Him.

The first step in deliverance is establishing friendship with God through obedience, submission, and reverence. The Bible tells us that "*the fear of the Lord is the beginning of wisdom.*" When you submit to God fully, you allow Him to take charge and control of your life. When He is in control, the work of deliverance is not tricky. It becomes hard only when we attempt to do it independently without submitting to the Lord.

Once you've submitted, repentance will follow. Cry out to God, saying, "*God, I see the sins of my forefathers. I repent and ask for mercy.*" Exodus 34:7 states that God visits the iniquity of the fathers upon the children to the third and fourth generations. You may wonder how you can identify sin in your foundation. Look at your dreams. Your dream life reveals much about your spiritual state, but if the enemy has shut down your dream land, and prevents you from seeing what he is doing. 90% of what you dream is related to your foundation. If you consistently dream of kingdoms, like the witchcraft kingdom, marine kingdom, or serpentine spirits, or if you dream of spirit spouses, mermaids, graveyard spirits, or interactions with the dead, these indicate that there is sin in your foundation that has yet to be dealt with.

The most difficult powers to uproot are the foundational ones. This is why you should not take your foundation lightly. The other 10% of your battles are usually due to worldly influences—arrows from relationships with satanic agents or external spiritual attacks. These are easier to deal with, but foundational issues require discipline and a long journey of deliverance. However, as you progress in foundation deliverance, you'll begin to see changes in your own life and that of your entire family. The chains will be broken, and those spirits will leave you.

Covenants exist in the foundation, so it's vital to stay close to God, cultivate a relationship with Him, and live by His laws. Only then will you receive the supernatural wisdom to tackle this journey. Even after receiving Jesus, it's crucial to revisit your life and check for any negative patterns. These must be dealt with if you wish to experience the release that comes through the power of Christ.

Jesus told his disciples not to leave Jerusalem until they received the Holy Spirit (Acts 1:4-5). You cannot face these strong, stubborn powers without the fire of God. They have been in place for so long, backed by legal covenants, that divine power is required to overcome them.

Unfortunately, the journey of deliverance is not an easy one. It doesn't matter what rank or qualifications you have;

deliverance requires a person to sit down and revisit their foundation, step by step. Deliverance has no respect for ranks, fame, and age. But it becomes much easier once you start doing the right thing. Repentance is crucial. When there is sin, it creates a blockage between you and the Spirit of God. When you pray, your prayers may not reach heaven because the heavens are shut and bouncing back. Repentance breaks that wall down like the walls of Jericho and opens the sky. Once the power of sin is broken, you have access to God.

Forgiveness is another critical component of deliverance. You must forgive everyone, whether you feel they are right or wrong. Forgiveness is for your benefit, not theirs. You don't need to go back to the person who wronged you. Forgiveness is about releasing them from your heart without anger, malice, or grudges. This ensures there is no legal covenant preventing your deliverance.

Once you have repented and forgiven, you are transformed from darkness to light. God becomes your friend, and as you walk in alignment with Him through His commandments, the sin that once held you down will begin to break. It's all about spiritual kingdoms the demonic kingdoms will fall one by one, as there is no longer a legal right for them to hold you captive. God is a just judge, and His judgment will fall upon them if they resist after you have repented, forgiven, renounced, and rejected them.

If they continue being stubborn after all these steps, another option is to take them to the Court of Heaven and seek a verdict. This is all about sin and repentance.

The beautiful thing is that when you take these steps, the deliverance is not just for you, but for your entire foundation, family tree, bloodline, your entire generation as well as the Church and the Nation. Everyone connected to you will experience freedom. For example, if there were spirit spouses in your family, those spirits affected everyone, mother, grandmother, etc. But once one person rises to take them down, everyone will be released. You have the authority to break those chains, and as you do, others will begin to see relief, one kingdom after another, all because of your obedience.

Therefore, we must keep our heavens open. We must stay in constant communion with God, hearing His voice through His Word. That is our greatest weapon the voice of God. You cannot be delivered if you don't hear His voice. His voice is in His Word. Stay spirit-filled and remain consistent in prayer and the Word of God. To all stubborn enemies that you have experienced from the beginning of this book till now, enemies who have vowed that no matter what you do, they will not let your foundation, your people, go! It is now time to drag all of them to the courts of heaven.

Be specific, what is your petition? You must have done everything we have discussed from the beginning of this book. This includes mainly removing legal rights by confession, repentance, renouncing, cleansing, forgiveness, consecration, and ensuring you've prayed and fasted appropriately. Before you drag the enemy to the Courts of Heaven, you must ensure that your matter is clean, for the accuser of the brethren will not find a ground for accusation.

The Bible also says, "*Submit to the Lord, resist the devil, and he will flee from you.*" You are living a life of fearing the Lord, submitting to Him, and resisting the devil. But if the devil does not seem to leave you, it's time to take the case to the Courts of Heaven. In other words, the enemy will not find you guilty of anything. What you're seeking in the Courts of Heaven is a verdict. If they find you guilty of anything, you will lose. It's just like a regular court here on Earth.

Understanding the Courts of Heaven: Protocols and Scriptural Alignment

In matters concerning the Courts of Heaven, it's imperative to discern which court you're accessing to ensure adherence to proper protocols and jurisdiction. Engaging with the appropriate court is crucial for the validity of your case. Moreover, all petitions and proceedings must be grounded in Scripture; praying without scriptural backing is ineffective and unfruitful.

Within the Courts of Heaven, our role is not merely to pray but to legislate. We present cases, submit petitions, seek judgments, and request documentation for all proceedings. This process requires a deep understanding of divine justice and the legal frameworks established by God's Word.

Approaching the Courts of Heaven necessitates a posture of humility, repentance, and unwavering faith in the finished work of Christ. Only through His sacrifice do we have standing before the righteous Judge. Therefore, it's essential to ensure that all actions within the heavenly courts are in full alignment with biblical principles and the leading of the Holy Spirit

There are five courts of heaven, and how to utilize them without compromising:

What are the five Courts of Heaven?

1. Court of Partition
2. Court of Judgement
3. Court of Accusation
4. Court of Redemption
5. Court of Yahweh

1. COURTS OF PERTITION;

-The Jurisdiction of the courts of partition; Believers bring their requests, needs, and desires before God.

-Request for guidance and direction, Intercession for others, Prayers for provision, prayers for protection, prayers for blessings.

Let's Pray;

Father God, my just Judge, I ask the court of Petition to be open for me, seeking guidance, direction, provision, protection, and blessings.

Pray: Father God, today in the name of Jesus, I come into the courts of petition, seeking your intervention for guidance, provision, protection, and blessing.

How do we approach the courts of petition?

a) Approach courts with thanksgiving
b) Present the request with specificity
c) Prayers with faith and expectation
d) Align petition with God's will
e) Persist in prayer until a breakthrough

a) Approach courts with thanksgiving

Psalms 100:4 calls for entering God's gates with thanksgiving and His courts with praise

Pray: Open your mouth and begin to thank the Lord. Thank the Lord for everything, answered prayers, even unanswered prayers, for Thanksgiving is a passcode for more open heaven.

b) Present the request with specificity

Philippians 4:6 encourages believers not to be anxious about anything, but to address every situation with prayer, supplication, and thanksgiving

Pray: Father, I pray in the name of Jesus and I receive the grace to pray and address everything with prayer, supplication, and thanksgiving

c) Prayers with faith and expectation

Mark 11:24 says "Therefore, I tell you, whatever you ask for in prayer, believe that you have received it, and it will be yours

Pray: My Father and my God, every unanswered prayer that has robbed my Faith, I recover my Faith back in the name of Jesus

Pray: Today I believe again, everything I ever prayed to God for, I believe it, I receive it, it is mine in the name of Jesus

d) Align petition with God's will

1 John 5:14-15 says we have confidence in God because if we ask anything according to His will, He hears us. If we know He hears us, we know we have what we asked for.

Pray: Spirit of the living God, arrest my Soul, My Spirit, and my body, within the will of God, in the name of Jesus.

e) Persist in prayer until breakthrough

Luke 18:1-8 mentions the parable of the persistent widow found in Luke 18 showcases *how our petitions to God deepen our relationship with Him.*

·Biblical examples of the courts of petition;

-Hannah's petition for a Son, Prophet Samuel

Key Lessons from Hannah's Petition: 1 Samuel 1: 10-18

1. Honest prayer: She prayed from the depths of her sorrow.
2. Persistence: She didn't give up despite years of barrenness and mockery.
3. Faith with a vow: She made a sincere vow and kept it.
4. Trust in God's timing: She left her burden with God and was no longer downcast.

-Solomon's Partition to God, requesting for wisdom

1 Kings 3: 3-15

Key Lessons from Solomon's Petition:

1. Humility: Solomon acknowledged his limitations.
2. Priorities: He valued wisdom and justice over personal gain.
3. Alignment with God's purpose: His request was centered on serving others.
4. God's generosity: God honors selfless, purposeful prayers.

Solomon's petition to God is beautifully recorded in 1 Kings 3:3–15, shortly after he became king of Israel. This moment is often referred to as Solomon's prayer for wisdom.

-Nehemiah's petition for Jerusalem, Nehemiah 1-2

Key Lessons from Nehemiah's Petition Nehemiah 1: 5-12

1. Start with worship before making requests.
2. Own personal and communal responsibility for sin.
3. Anchor your prayers in God's Word and promises.
4. Pray with purpose Nehemiah prayed because he planned to act.
5. Combine prayer with planning Nehemiah didn't just pray; he prepared to rebuild.

-The early Church's prayer for boldness

Acts 4: 23-31

Key Lessons from the Early Church's Prayer (Acts 4:24–30)

1. They focused on God's sovereignty, not their fear.
2. They anchored their prayer in Scripture.
3. They asked for boldness, not protection.
4. They prayed as a united community.
5. God answered immediately and powerfully.

Travailing in Prayer;

What Does "Travailing in Prayer" Mean?

The term "travail" is often associated with childbirth (e.g., Isaiah 66:8, Galatians 4:19), symbolizing the pain, persistence, and focused effort required to bring something forth.

Galatians 4:19:

"My little children, of whom I travail in birth again until Christ be formed in you."

In prayer, travailing means:

1. Groaning or weeping under a deep burden.
2. Laboring spiritually until there's a breakthrough.
3. Intense intercession often inspired by the Holy Spirit.

Romans 8:26

"The Spirit itself maketh intercession for us with groanings which cannot be uttered.

How to Travail in Prayer?

Step-by-Step:

1. Be Filled with the Spirit

Travailing prayer is often Spirit-led. Begin by surrendering and asking the Holy Spirit to guide your prayer.

2. Enter a Place of Solitude

This kind of prayer may involve crying, groaning, or extended time. Find a private space where you can fully engage with God without distraction.

3. Pray the Word of God

Let your burden align with God's will. Use Scripture to frame your intercession.

4. Yield to the Burden

You may feel a weight or urgency on your heart. Let it drive your prayer this might include tears, moaning, or simply silent weeping.

1. Persist Until Release

Just like labor, travailing prayer continues until there's a sense of breakthrough, peace, or clarity.

Advantages of Travailing in Prayer

1. Spiritual Breakthrough:

Travailing often precedes revival, healing, or deliverance. You're pushing through spiritual resistance.

Isaiah 66:8

"As soon as Zion travailed, she brought forth her children."

2. Deeper Intimacy with God

This kind of prayer leads you beyond surface-level communication into deep communion with God.

3. Birth of God's Purposes

Many revivals, ministries, or personal transformations begin with someone travailing in prayer. You're birthing God's will on earth.

4. Holy Spirit Empowerment

It teaches dependence on the Spirit's help in prayer, especially when words fail.

Romans 8:26

5. Spiritual Growth

You grow in sensitivity, spiritual authority, and understanding of God's heart.

Requests from God for Spiritual Gifts and Empowerment

Pray to Activate Spiritual Gifts;

1. Focus: Seek the activation and manifestation of spiritual gifts within your life
2. Scripture: 1 Corinthians 12:7 "Now to each one the manifestation of the Spirit is given for the common good."
3. Prayer: "Holy Spirit, activate the gifts You have placed within me. Grant me the wisdom to use them for the edification of the Church and the fulfillment of Your Kingdom purposes. Amen."

Prayer for Empowerment for Service;

1. Focus: Request empowerment to serve effectively in God's Kingdom.
2. Scripture: Acts 1:8 "But you will receive power when the Holy Spirit comes on you; and you will be my witnesses."
3. Prayer: "Father, empower me with Your Holy Spirit to serve faithfully and effectively. Equip me to be a witness of Your love and truth in all that I do. Amen."

Prayer for Boldness and Courage;

1. Focus: Ask for boldness to step out in faith and courage to fulfill your divine assignment.

2. Scripture: 2 Timothy 1:7 – "For the Spirit God gave us does not make us timid, but gives us power, love, and self-discipline."
3. Prayer: "Lord, fill me with boldness and courage to step into the assignments You've prepared for me. Remove all fear and replace it with unwavering faith in Your ability to work through me. Amen."

How can a believer Sustain Spiritual Empowerment?

1. Regular Fellowship: Continue to engage with fellow believers through church services, small groups, and community events.
2. Continuous Learning: Study Scripture and teachings that deepen your understanding of spiritual gifts and empowerment.
3. Service: Actively serve in areas where your gifts can be utilized, such as ministry, outreach, or support roles.
4. Reflection: Regularly assess your spiritual growth and areas where you can further yield to the Holy Spirit's work.

Pray:

Heavenly Father, I come before You with a humble heart, asking for the gifts of Your Spirit, not for my glory but for the building up of Your Church and the advancement of Your Kingdom. Lord, I ask for spiritual gift and empowerment, I ask for: Wisdom, knowledge, faith, healing, miracles, prophecy, discernment, speaking in tongues, and interpretation of tongues, In the name of Jesus. (James 1:5, 1 Corinthians 12:8, 1 Corinthians 12:9, Mark 16:18, 1 Corinthians 12:10, 1 Corinthians 14:1, 1 Corinthians 12:10).

Pray:

Holy Spirit, fill me afresh. Let Your gifts operate in me according to Your will and for Your glory. Help me walk in love, the greatest gift of all. In Jesus' mighty name, Amen.

2. THE COURT OF JUDGEMENT;

This is where legal matters are decided according to God's law and righteousness. This court renders a verdict, establishes justice, and issues decrees.

Jurisdictions are: disputes between believers, injustice and oppression, territorial conflicts, legal matters in the spirit realm, divine verdicts and decrees.

How do we approach the courts of Judgement?

a) Present your case with evidence;

b) Appeal to God's written words

c).Base argument on covenant promises;

d).Request righteous Judgement;

e).Accept and enforce the verdict

a)Present your case with evidence;

Isaiah 43: 26

Put me in remembrance; let us argue together; set forth your case, that you may be proved right.

Pray;

"Lord, help me to remember Your promises and truth in every situation. I invite You to argue my case and defend me before every accusation. Let Your justice prevails and prove me right in every challenge I face. Amen."

b)Appeal to God's written words;

Psalms 119: 89 *"Your word, Lord, is eternal; it stands firm in the heavens*

Pray;

"Lord, your word is eternal and unchanging. Let Your promises stand firm over my life forever. Help me to trust in Your faithfulness and live according to Your statutes every day. Amen."

c) Base argument on covenant promises;

Psalms 105: 8-11 These verses praise God for faithfully remembering His covenant with His people. It recalls His promise to Abraham, Isaac, and Jacob, confirming it as an everlasting agreement to give their descendants the land of Canaan as their inheritance.

Pray:

Heavenly Father, thank You for being a covenant-keeping God. Just as You remembered Your promise to Abraham, Isaac, and Jacob, I pray that You will remember and fulfill every covenant promise You have made concerning my life and my family. Let Your everlasting Word guide us into the inheritance You have prepared for us, in Jesus' name. Amen.

d)Request righteous Judgement;

Psalm 7:6-11. The psalmist (David) calls on God to rise in anger against the wicked and bring justice. He asks God to judge fairly and defend the righteous. David affirms that God examines hearts and minds and is a righteous judge who protects those who are upright. He trusts in God's justice to punish evil and uphold the innocent.

Pray;

Righteous Judge, arise and bring justice in every area where wickedness prevails. Search my heart, O God, and find me upright before You. Defend me against those who do evil, and let Your justice prevail in my life, for I trust in Your perfect judgment and protection, in Jesus' name. Amen.

e) Accept and enforce the verdict

Daniel 7: 22 *Until the Ancient of Days came and pronounced judgment in favor of the holy people of the Highest, and the time came when they possessed the kingdom.*

Pray:

Ancient of Days, arise and pronounce judgment in my favor. Let every delay be broken, and bring me into the fullness of the kingdom You have prepared for Your holy people. Let this be the set time for me to possess my inheritance, in Jesus' name. Amen.

Biblical example of the Court of Judgment;

Solomon's Judgement between two mothers; (1 Kings 3:16-28),

Two women came to King Solomon, both claiming to be the mother of the same baby. Each said the other woman's baby had died and that the living child was hers. Solomon proposed to cut the baby in two and give each woman half. One woman agreed, but the other begged Solomon to give the baby to the other woman to save its life. Solomon then declared the woman who showed compassion to be the real mother and gave her the baby, demonstrating his great wisdom.

Daniels's appeal for Israel's restoration (Daniel 9)

In Daniel 9, Daniel prays earnestly to God after realizing from Scripture that Israel's exile would last 70 years. He confesses the nation's sins, acknowledges God's righteousness, and pleads for mercy and forgiveness. Daniel asks God to restore Jerusalem and the temple for His name's sake. In response, the angel Gabriel appears and gives Daniel a prophecy about the future, including the coming of the Anointed One and the eventual fulfillment of God's plan for Israel.

· ## Jesus' confrontation with Satan's accusations (Mathew 4:1-11)

After His baptism, Jesus was led into the wilderness where He fasted for 40 days. Satan tempted Him three times: to turn stones into bread, to throw Himself from the temple to test God, and to worship Satan in exchange for the world's kingdoms. Each time, Jesus resisted by quoting Scripture. Finally, He commanded Satan to leave, and the devil departed. Angels then came and cared for Him. This passage shows Jesus' faithfulness, strength, and reliance on God's Word to overcome temptation.

· ## The martyrs' cry for justice (Revelation 6: 9-11)

In this passage, John sees a vision of the souls of martyrs under the altar who were killed for their faith and testimony. They cry out to God, asking how long until He judges and avenges their deaths. They are each given white robes and told to rest a little longer until the full number of fellow servants and believers are also martyred. This symbolizes God's awareness of their suffering and His promise of eventual justice.

Travailing in Prayer;

· Ask God to judge areas of compromise in the Family, Church, and Community

Pray;

"Lord God, righteous and holy, we come before You with humble hearts, asking You to examine Your Church. Reveal the areas where we have compromised truth, allowed sin, or strayed from Your Word. Judge us in mercy and lead us to repentance. Purify Your Bride, Lord, and restore holiness, unity, and love for Your truth. Raise up leaders and believers who will stand firm in faith, and help us to walk in obedience. In Jesus' name, Amen." (Psalm 139:23, 1 Peter 4:17, Revelation 2:4–5, Psalm 119:105, Psalm 145:8, Revelation 3:19)

This kind of prayer is meant to invite God's correction and cleansing, not out of condemnation, but out of a desire for the Church to be fully aligned with His will.

· Seek a verdict against spiritual strongholds in communities;

Pray;

"Righteous Judge of all the earth, we come before You on behalf of our community. We ask for Your verdict against every spiritual stronghold of darkness, deception, addiction, violence, and oppression that is holding people captive. Expose the enemy's schemes and render judgment in favor of Your Kingdom. Let truth, righteousness, and peace be established. We plead the blood of Jesus over this land and declare freedom in His name. Break every chain and raise up a people devoted to You. In Jesus' mighty name, Amen." (Genesis 18:25, 2 Corinthians 10:4, Isaiah 61:1, Luke 8:17, Daniel 7:22). "Let truth, righteousness, and peace be established.

· Petition for the enforcement of Christ's victory over darkness.

Pray:

"Lord Jesus, we thank You for Your victory on the cross. You disarmed the powers of darkness and triumphed over them. We now petition You, Righteous King, to enforce that victory in every place where darkness still reigns. Break chains of addiction, oppression, and fear. Let every lie of the enemy be exposed by Your truth. We declare that every knee must bow to You, and every stronghold must fall. Let Your light shine and Your Kingdom come. In Jesus' powerful name, Amen." (Colossians 2:15, Luke 10:19, Ephesians 6:12)

3. THE COURT OF ACCUSATION

This is where Satan brings charges against believers; this court addresses allegations, condemnations, and spiritual warfare.

Jurisdictions; When there are generational issues and curses, legal rights claimed by the enemy, demonic oppression, and harassment.

How do we approach the courts of accusations?

    a) Acknowledge genuine sin and repent;

    b) Apply the blood of Jesus as your defense;

    c) Present evidence of your redemption

    d) Refute false accusations with truth;

    e) Stand on your position in Christ

a) Acknowledge genuine sin and repent;

John 1:9

If we confess our sins, he is faithful and just to forgive us *our* sins, and to cleanse us from all unrighteousness.

Pray;

Lord Jesus, you are the true light that gives light to everyone. Shine Your light into every dark area of my life. Guide my steps, remove all confusion, and help me walk in Your truth and clarity, in Jesus' name. Amen.

b) Apply the blood of Jesus as your defense;

Revelation 12:11

And they have defeated him by the blood of the Lamb and by their testimony. And they did not love their lives so much that they were afraid to die

Pray;

Heavenly Father, I declare victory through the blood of the Lamb and the word of my testimony. Strengthen my faith to stand firm, and help me to overcome every attack of the enemy by Your power and truth, in Jesus' name. Amen.

c) Present evidence of your redemption

Colossians 2:13-15

[13] When you were dead in your sins and in the uncircumcision of your flesh, God made you[a] alive with Christ. He forgave us all our sins, [14] having canceled the charge of our legal indebtedness, which stood against us and condemned us; he has taken it away, nailing it to the cross. [15] And having disarmed the powers and authorities, he made a public spectacle of them, triumphing over them by the cross

Pray;

Lord Jesus, thank You for forgiving all my sins and cancelling every record of debt against me. I praise You for triumphing over every power and authority on my behalf. Help me to walk in the freedom and victory You have won for me, in Jesus' name. Amen.

d) Refute false accusations with truth;

Isaiah 54:17

No weapon that is fashioned against you shall succeed, and you shall refute every tongue that rises against you in judgment. This is the heritage of the servants of the LORD and their vindication from me, declares the LORD.

Pray;

Lord, I thank You that no weapon formed against me shall prosper. I condemn every tongue that rises against me in judgment. Let Your divine protection surrounds me, and let Your righteousness defend and establish me, in Jesus' name. Amen.

e) Stand on your position in Christ;

Romans 8:33-34

"Who will bring any charge against God's elect?" and answers that "it is God who justifies." Then, it asks: "Who is the one who condemns?" and answers that it is "Christ Jesus who died, more than that, who was raised to life, and is at the right hand of God, and is also interceding for us.

Pray;

Father, thank You that no accusation can stand against me because Christ Jesus intercedes on my behalf. I stand confident in Your grace and protection, knowing I am justified and accepted in Your sight, in Jesus' name. Amen.

Biblical examples;

Satan's accusations of Job;

Job 1-2

Job, a righteous and wealthy man, loses his children and possessions after Satan challenges his faithfulness. Despite his losses, Job worships God. In a second test, Satan afflicts Job with painful sores. Even then, Job remains faithful, refusing to curse God. His three friends come to mourn with him in silence.

Joshua, the High Priest, before the Angel;

Zechariah 3:1-5

The prophet sees Joshua the high priest standing before God, with Satan accusing him. God rebukes Satan and declares Joshua forgiven. Joshua's filthy clothes are removed and replaced with clean garments, symbolizing God's cleansing and restoration.

The woman caught in adultery;

John 8:1-11

Jesus forgives a woman caught in adultery and tells her to sin no more, after challenging her accusers to judge only if they are without sin.

Paul's thorn in the flesh;

2 Corinthians 12:7-10

Paul speaks of a "thorn in the flesh" given to keep him humble. Though he asked God to remove it, God told him,

"My grace is sufficient for you." Paul then rejoices in weakness, knowing God's power is made perfect in it.

Travailing in Prayer; In this court of accusation, we enter the courts with repentance.

Pray;

Righteous Judge, as I enter Your courts, I come with a heart of repentance. Wash me clean, O Lord, and silence every accusation of the enemy with the blood of Jesus. Let Your mercy speak for me, and restore me to right standing before You, in Jesus' name. Amen.

Repent of personal and corporate sin, silence the enemy's accusations through praise and declarations, apply the blood of Jesus to areas of vulnerability.

Pray;

Father, I repent of all personal and corporate sins. I silence every enemy accusation through praise and bold declarations of Your truth. By the power of the blood of Jesus, I cover every area of my life that is vulnerable, declaring protection, healing, and victory in Jesus' name. Amen.

4. THE COURT OF REDEMPTION

This court deals with matters of Salvation, restoration, and application of Christ's finished work. This Court addresses the legal transfer of ownership from darkness to light.

Jurisdiction; Salvation and regeneration, deliverance from bondage, recovery of lost inheritance, restoration of relationships, healing of body, soul, and spirit.

How do we approach the courts of redemption?

    a) Present the blood of Jesus as payment;

    b) Claim your rights as a redeemed child;

    c) Appeal to Christ as your advocate;

    d) Request restoration of what was stolen;

    e) Accept your new identity in Christ;

a)Present the blood of Jesus as payment;

Ephesian 1:7

"In Him we have redemption through His blood, the forgiveness of sins, according to the riches of His grace."

Pray;

Lord Jesus, thank You for redeeming me through Your precious blood. I receive the forgiveness of my sins and walk in the freedom and grace You have richly provided. Let Your mercy continually speak for me, in Jesus' name. Amen.

    b) Claim your rights as a redeemed child;

Galatians 4:4-7

[4] But when the fullness of time had come, God sent forth his Son, born of woman, born under the law, [5] to redeem those who were under the law, so that we might receive adoption as sons. [6] And because you are sons, God has sent the Spirit of his Son into our hearts, crying, "Abba! Father!" [7] So you are no longer a slave, but a son, and if a son, then an heir through God.

Pray:

Heavenly Father, thank You for sending Your Son to redeem me and make me Your child. By Your Spirit, I cry out, "Abba, Father." Help me walk in the full rights and inheritance I have as Your heir, in Jesus' name. Amen.

c) Appeal to Christ as your advocate;

1 John 2:1

"My dear children, I write this to you so that you will not sin. But if anyone does sin, we have an advocate with the Father, Jesus Christ, the Righteous One

Pray;

Father, thank You for giving me, Jesus Christ, my Advocate with You. When I fall, remind me of Your mercy and lead me to repentance. Strengthen me to walk in obedience and keep me from sin, in Jesus' name. Amen.

d) Request restoration of what was stolen.

Joel 2:25

"I will repay you for the years the locusts have eaten - the great locust and the young locust, the other locusts and the locust swarm - my great army that I sent among you

Pray:

Lord, I thank You for Your promise to restore what was lost. I pray that You will redeem every wasted year and heal every area of loss in my life. Let restoration flow according to Your word, in Jesus' name. Amen.

e) Accept your new identity in Christ;

2 Corinthians 5:17

Therefore, if anyone is in Christ, he is a new creation. The old has passed away; behold, the new has come

Pray;

Father, thank You that in Christ I am a new creation. I let go of the old and embrace the new life You have given me. Help me to walk daily in the freedom, identity, and purpose found in You, in Jesus' name. Amen.

Biblical examples;

Ruth and Boaz at the city gate;

Ruth 4

The summary of Ruth Chapter four, Boaz redeems Ruth by marrying her, securing her and Naomi's future. Their union leads to the birth of Obed, grandfather of King David, showing God's faithfulness in restoring and blessing.

The Prodigal Son's restoration;

Luke 15:11-32

The summary of this passage that a younger son asks for his inheritance early, wastes it in reckless living, and ends up destitute. He returns home repentant, and his father warmly welcomes him back with forgiveness and celebration. The older son struggles with jealousy, but the father reminds him of the joy in restoring what was lost.

The Gadarene demonic deliverance;

Mark 5: 1-20

Jesus heals a man possessed by many demons in the region of the Gerasene's. The demons leave the man and enter a herd of pigs, which rush into the sea and drown. The healed man wants to follow Jesus, but Jesus sends him to share his testimony with others.

Paul's convention and calling;

Acts 9

The summary of this passage, Saul, a fierce persecutor of Christians, encounters Jesus on the road to Damascus and is dramatically converted. He is blinded, then healed by

Ananias, receives the Holy Spirit, and begins boldly preaching that Jesus is the Son of God.

Travailing in Prayer: Reclaim the aspect of your calling that has been dormant, seek restoration of broken relationships within the body, and activate spiritual gifts that have been neglected

Pray;

Lord, I come before You in prayer, asking for revival in my calling. Rekindle the fire in every dormant area of my life and restore all broken relationships within Your body. Activate and empower every spiritual gift within me that has been neglected, that I may serve You fully and effectively, in Jesus' name. Amen.

5. THE COURT OF YAWHEH.

This is the Court of the Lord. This is the highest court representing direct access to God's throne. This court deals with matters of worship, fellowship and divine purpose.

Jurisdiction; Divine encounters, revelation, worship, and communion with God. Commissioning and calling. Covenant establishment. Ultimate authority and sovereignty.

How do we approach the courts of YAHWEH?

a) . We enter this Court with reverence and holy fear
b) . Approach through the blood of Jesus
c) Come with clean hands and pure hearts
d) Wait in His presence with a surrendered will
e) Receive His word with obedience;

a)We enter in this Court with reverence and holy fear;

Hebrews 12:28-29

Therefore, since we are receiving a kingdom that cannot be shaken, let us be thankful, and so worship God acceptably with reverence and awe, [29] for our "God is a consuming fire.

Pray;

Father, help me to serve You with reverence and awe, fully aware of Your holy presence. Teach me to honor You with a sincere heart, knowing that You are a consuming fire who purifies and refines me, in Jesus' name. Amen.

b) Approach through the blood of Jesus;

Hebrews 10: 19-22

Therefore, brothers and sisters, since we have confidence to enter the Most Holy Place by the blood of Jesus, [20] by a new and living way opened for us through the curtain, that is, his body, [21] and since we have a great priest over the house of God, [22] let us draw near to God with a sincere heart and with the full assurance that faith brings, having our hearts sprinkled to cleanse us from a guilty conscience and having our bodies washed with pure water.

Pray;

Lord, thank You for the confidence to enter Your presence boldly through the blood of Jesus. Help me to draw near with a sincere heart, full of faith and purity, cleansing my conscience from all guilt, and holding fast to the hope You have given me, in Jesus' name. Amen.

c) Come with clean hands and pure hearts;

Psalms 24: 3-4

Who shall ascend into the hill of the LORD? or who shall stand in his holy place? He that hath clean hands, and a pure heart; who hath not lifted up

Pray;

Lord, create in me a clean heart and pure hands. Help me to live a blameless life so that I may stand worthy to enter Your holy presence. May my soul seek after You sincerely, in Jesus' name. Amen.

d) Wait in His presence with a surrendered will;

Isaiah 6:8

Then I heard the voice of the Lord saying, "Whom shall I send? And who will go for us? " And I said, "Here am I. Send me!"

Pray;

Here I am, Lord; send me! I am willing and ready to answer Your call. Use me for Your purpose and guide me in every step, in Jesus' name. Amen.

e) Receive His word with obedience;

1 Samuel 3:10

The LORD came and stood there, calling as at the other times, "Samuel! Samuel!" Then Samuel said, "Speak, for your servant is listening."

Pray;

Lord, speak to me clearly as You did to Samuel. Help me to recognize Your voice and respond obediently whenever You call. Open my heart to hear Your guidance daily, in Jesus' name. Amen.

Biblical examples;

Moses on Mount Sinai; Exodus 24: 15-18

When Moses went up on the mountain, the cloud covered it, ¹⁶ and the glory of the LORD settled on Mount Sinai. For six days, the cloud covered the mountain, and on the seventh day the LORD called to Moses from within the cloud. ¹⁷ To the Israelites the glory of the LORD looked like a consuming fire on top of the mountain. ¹⁸ Then Moses entered the cloud as he went up the mountain. And he stayed on the mountain forty days and forty nights.

Isaiah's vision in the temple; Isaiah 6

In summary, this chapter, Isaiah has a vision of God's glory in the temple. He feels unworthy but is purified by a burning coal from the altar. When God asks, "Who will go for us?" Isaiah volunteers to be His messenger, ready to deliver God's message to the people.

The transfiguration of Jesus; Matthew 17: 1-8

Jesus is transfigured before Peter, James, and John on a high mountain. His face shines like the sun, and His clothes become dazzling white. Moses and Elijah appear and speak with Him. A voice from a bright cloud declares, "This is My beloved Son... listen to Him!" The disciples fall into fear, but Jesus reassures them.

John's vision on Patmos;

Revelation 4-5

Chapter   4:
John is taken in a vision to God's heavenly throne room. He sees God's glory, surrounded by 24 elders and four living creatures who worship Him continually, declaring His holiness and power as Creator.

Chapter   5:
John sees a scroll in God's hand that no one can open until

the Lamb (Jesus), who was slain, is found worthy. Heaven erupts in worship, praising the Lamb for redeeming people from every nation and making them a kingdom and priests to God.

Travailing in prayer;

Set aside extended times of worship and waiting, seek fresh revelations of God's heart and plans, position yourself to receive Pentecostal empowerment.

Pray;

Father, I set aside this time to worship and wait in Your presence. Reveal more of Your heart and Your divine plans for my life. Position me, Lord, to receive a fresh outpouring of Your Spirit, empower me anew, just as You did at Pentecost, in Jesus' name. Amen.

Throughout my journey of deep deliverance, I have utilized all these courts. I have travailed with knowledge, without overstepping any spiritual jurisdiction. Deep deliverance requires knowledge, understanding, wisdom, obedience, and humility before the Lord; only then can God truly help us. It is not possible to pursue deep deliverance alone. God seeks a willing vessel, led by the Holy Spirit, to carry out this work and rescue souls who are in deep spiritual torment, crying out daily, "Abba."

Today, I am happy to say that my family has experienced the mercies of God through laboring in prayer. In Colossians 4:12, Paul mentions Epaphras as one who is *"always laboring fervently for you in his prayers."* Likewise, we have witnessed restoration in nearly every area of our foundation, bloodline, family tree, and household. Most importantly, the greatest breakthrough has been salvation and revival many have turned to Jesus and are now faithfully serving Jesus Christ of Nazareth.

Through this Journey of deliverance, I have learned that the True church of Christ is not as easy as we all knew. God said Be ye holy as I am holy. For believers to be able to find heaven, they will require many to find the true Christ through confession, repentance, renunciation, obedience, purity, holiness, and righteousness. Otherwise, Heaven is far from many of us, even though we are still in church proclaiming Jesus and reading the bible from Genesis to Revelation. *Mathew 7:13 "You can enter God's Kingdom only through the narrow gate. The highway to hell is broad, and its gate is wide for the many who choose that way.*

This process is meant for spiritually mature individuals. You cannot just say, "*I'm going to the Courts of Heaven.*" Spiritual maturity is essential because it requires having walked the journey of deliverance, ensuring everything is in order. When you've done everything, and it still seems like you are not entirely delivered—when there are still things that you don't understand here and there—then it's time to approach the Courts of Heaven. By this point, many of the spirits, demons, and powers of darkness might have already left, but you may still sense something lingering that keeps coming back, even though you think you are delivered. This is when you must access the Courts of Heaven.

At this point, you must understand you are entering into another spiritual dimension, a realm where you will acquire results because you're stepping into a higher judicial realm in the spirit. The first step is to cleanse your bloodline. In deliverance, the power will challenge you if anything in your bloodline has made a demonic covenant. This is why we access the blood of Jesus. As I mentioned, you've already done most of this by applying the blood of Jesus, but you might still see things happening.

For example, demons that are assigned to dry up your money, dry up your marriage, your spiritual life, or dry up your family may be operating through a demonic covenant. If you find yourself in this situation, it doesn't matter how educated you are, how business-minded you are, or how hard you work. If this demonic force is sucking everything dry, you will find yourself exhausted. This is when this spirit needs to be addressed in the Courts of Heaven.

You can pray:

"Father, I come to You, and I ask for the blood of Jesus to cleanse my bloodline and remove all demonic covenants, as Hebrews 12:24 says. Let the blood of Jesus break any covenant that holds me and my lineage. I stand in the gap for my family members—my parents, siblings, and children. I repent on behalf of my family, and I ask for the blood of Jesus to cleanse them."

Sometimes, legal covenants are formed through curses. For example, if you've cursed your spouse, children, or others, those words can form legal covenants. You must repent and ask God to break those legal claims. Pray:

"Father, I repent for every word I have spoken against my husband, wife, children, parents, congregation, or pastor. I ask for the blood of Jesus to nullify every negative word I've spoken, whether I was aware of it or not. Let every right the enemy claims be revoked now in the name of Jesus."

Then, you move into prophesying life into your circumstances. As it is written in Daniel 7:10, the court is seated, and the books are opened. Hebrews 10:19 tells us that when we enter the Holy of Holies by the blood of Jesus, we are qualified to step into the realm of the Spirit and access the books of Heaven. In this court, you stand by the Lord and proclaim His word.

You must ask, "*What is written in the book of Heaven about me?*" Begin to declare your destiny according to what is written in the book of Heaven. For example, if you have a prophecy that hasn't come to pass, begin to declare:

"Lord, I ask for wisdom, knowledge, favor, grace, and power to fulfill the purpose You have written in my book."

Then, even if your life isn't reflecting what is written in the book of Heaven, you must petition God. Ask for mercy and for God to reveal anything in your life that is hindering your destiny. Say:

"Lord, if anything is stopping Your purpose in my life or the lives of those I represent, I ask You to judge it now in the name of Jesus."

At this point, you may encounter resistance to your spiritual walk, family life, or other areas. If there are powers of darkness causing division in your family, ask God to judge them. Pray:

"Any resistance to my nuclear family, causing divorce, family separation, or chaos, I ask You, Lord, to judge it in the name of Jesus. I declare, like Joshua, as for me and my house, we will serve the Lord!"

Then, say:

"Lord, let everything written in the books of Heaven about my family begin to manifest now. Let everything be put in divine order. May the decisions and verdicts be rendered in Jesus' name."

You are standing in the Court of Heaven, petitioning for the release of God's written word about you and your family.

Approach the Court of Heaven from three areas: as a Father, as a Friend, and as a Judge.

1. **As a Father:** In Luke 11:1, Jesus's disciples asked Him, "*Lord, teach us to pray.*" Jesus's prayer life was powerful because He was communicating with His Father. You must also approach God as a loving Father, spending time in His presence.

2. **As a Friend:** In Luke 11:5-7, Jesus teaches a parable about a friend who asks for help at midnight. When you approach God as a friend, you enter the "*Council of the Lord,*" where you present your petitions to Him.

3. **As a Judge:** Finally, when you approach God as a Judge, you step into the Court of Heaven, where decisions are made regarding your life. Jeremiah 23:18 speaks of those who stand in the counsel of the Lord, hearing His word and marking it. This is where judgments are rendered for you.

After petitioning in all three dimensions (Father, Friend, and Judge), you must declare that the enemy has no legal right to oppose you. You can say:

"Lord Jesus, according to Colossians 2:14, every handwritten ordinance against me has been nailed to the cross. I declare that every issue, every stubborn attack against me and my family is broken in Jesus' name. Any legal covenant the enemy holds over my life is revoked now in Jesus' name."

At this point, you should expect to receive a release. You will experience a sense of peace and freedom when God's verdict is rendered. The enemy's strongholds will be broken, and you will feel lighter in spirit, soul, and body.

Remember, the Courts of Heaven are accessed by faith. You'll notice a tremendous sense of relief once you've gone through these steps. You will no longer experience the attacks you once did, and you'll feel lighter. This process works by faith and by the Spirit.

In conclusion, after following these steps and entering the Courts of Heaven, you will be released from the spiritual bondages that have held you back. God will respond to your petition whether you go individually or as a representative for a group or nation. You must continue to work hard, ensuring no legal right remains for the enemy. Light will come to your bloodline, your foundation, and your generation because you are called to be a burning and shining light (John 5:35).

Once you have gone through the Courts of Heaven, expect breakthroughs and answers to your prayers. The Lord is faithful, and His judgment will bring you freedom.

More deep Petitioning;

Another way to approach the Courts of Heaven is by petitioning. For example, if any dark kingdom remains stubborn, you can begin your approach by petitioning. You might say, "*Our Father, we are in a new season of appeal to the Court of Heaven against dark kingdom manipulation over the children of God. Many children of God have been manipulated. The strongman pursuing us, known as poverty, financial crisis, principalities, witchcraft, sorcery, diviners, wizards, warlocks, strongholds, and dark powers, must now bow down. Father, we have a divine assignment through intercessory prayer to bring Your purpose here on earth into fruition.*

Lord, we ask that, as we petition, those dark powers and principalities, witchcraft, and wizards who have been projecting sickness, infirmity, diseases, and incurable diseases like cancer, heart failure, liver failure, pancreatic diseases, or any other body system diseases upon the children of God, be confronted and disgraced. We ask that whatever accusation they have against Your children that grants them jurisdiction be nullified.

The strongman called Parax, the demon that is sucking everything out of our lives, must be judged, Lord, and its legal right removed. The Bible says, Father, that deliverance is the children's bread. When we repent of our sins, God is faithful in His mercy to deliver us completely. Father, let the strongman and the entire kingdom lose their legal right. Let the legal rights of the marine kingdom in our lives be removed. Let the legal rights of the water spirit in our lives be removed. Let the legal rights of witchcraft be removed. Let the legal rights of the serpentine kingdom be removed. Let the legal rights of spiritual marriages be removed. In Jesus' mighty name.

Father, in Jesus' name, according to Psalm 7:11, I approach You as a righteous Judge, and I ask for access to the courts—Courts of Grace and Mercy, Courts of Intercession, Courts of Destiny, Courts of Life, Courts of Divine DNA, Courts of Divine Medicine, and Cancellation. Father, may You summon to the Courts of Yeshua Hamashiach the Seven Spirits of God, according to Isaiah 11:1-3, and the Cloud of Witnesses, according to Hebrews 12:1-2.

Father, we petition You for all documents related to the witchcraft kingdom, the serpentine kingdom, the water spirit kingdom, the marine kingdom, and all their ramifications in our bloodline, DNA, and foundation. Father, we honor You as holy. Many of the courts include covenants or agreements made by our forefathers, all hell, trading floors, plagues, verdicts, judgments, the court of sickness, the court of cancer, incurable diseases, terminal diseases, and untimely death. Let the Court be in cohesion, according to Daniel 7:9-10.

Father, Your word declares that if I confess my sins, You are faithful and just to forgive me and cleanse me from all unrighteousness. The Bible says in 1 John 1:9, "Great Judge of the universe, there are many sins, iniquities, and transgressions that our forefathers have committed against You. We have committed violence and broken Your law." We recognize that sin has accumulated, causing our protective hedge to break down, and hell is breaking loose on us and our children. Demons, witches, and wizards are causing broken families and unfaithfulness within the ecclesia (the Church), resulting in broken children, the mingling of demons with humankind, and spiritual marriages that hinder divine marriages to Your children in the serpent and water spirit kingdoms.

We ask You, Lord, to present the accusations against us for Your evaluation. Abba, Father, we are guilty and plead for forgiveness and mercy. Matthew 5:25 states that we should be willing to settle with our adversary. Therefore, righteous Father, we agree with all accusations and ask to remove their verdict, death, punishment, and pollution.

Father, we also petition You for a special angel to rescue us and our bloodline from the principal demon of Parax, witchcraft, water spirits, marine powers, and witchcraft polygamy. Let their kingdom, network, sciences, scientific council, gods and goddesses, strongmen, strongwomen, jinxes, warlocks, wizards, and other entities or organizations be brought to justice. Holy Spirit, may any artificial material used by these kingdoms to cause sickness, infirmity, and disease be consumed by liquid fire. We ask that the kingdoms sharing our humanity be summoned to present the documents of rights to our ownership in the various compartments of our society.

Merciful God, the technologies militating against us are harmful to our health, leading to sickness, infirmity, disease, and premature death. Isaiah 53 provides the details as we pray for total liberation from all sickness and bondage. You bore our sins and carried our sorrows. This negativity has stolen our lives, Father. May we be compensated in Jesus' name.

I appeal to the Court of Cancellation and request that all files and records be erased, as instructed in Colossians 2:14-16. I petition for total desynchronization from all the above-mentioned negativity so that they no longer have control over us. May the court render a verdict, a restraining verdict. Thank You, Heavenly Father, in Jesus' name. Amen.

So, this is another way of approaching the Courts of Heaven. When I approached the Court of Heaven aggressively, I always did both approaches. And God is merciful. I remember once in the Courts of Heaven, I suddenly felt dizzy and could see the ground lifting. I was shaking. I believe I was conducting a broadcast during the Midnight Battle, and it's captured on the recording, which is available on YouTube. I will never forget it. These Courts of Heaven are potent sessions, and engaging in them means the enemy cannot persist. After that, there's no way. You will find that you receive what you've been crying out for and asking for. You'll come to a place of rest and deal only with minor matters, such as those arrows that fly by day and by night. But in pertaining with the foundation matters addressed, I believe you've closed many doors.

Chapter 17:
Praying Without Seeing Answers.

The Spirit of God took me to the case of the three Hebrew boys—Shadrach, Meshach, and Abednego—and the case of Daniel. Sometimes, when you are praying, especially when you've embarked on a journey of deep deliverance and uprooting deep-seated roots, this is the most challenging journey you will ever undertake. It requires serious commitment, sacrifice, purity, holiness, and righteousness. If I lined up 100 servants of God here, I could tell you that only a few have taken this route. Many have decided to serve the Lord without pursuing deliverance. That's why you see a lot of confusion in the Church today. It is the sacrifice needed to consecrate yourself for the people of God so they can be cleansed and set free. The life of consecration is not for many in the Church today, so we need God's grace to help us with this.

Deliverance is deep; it's a process, a journey. It's not easy. It's like swimming in the middle of battles; you are all alone. This is where many people find themselves in the middle of nowhere, crying in the middle of the night, asking, *"God, are You still there? Are you still with me? Or am I just alone?"* At this point, you've already done all the right things. You're not an immature believer. You've passed that point; you're high above. You usually won't face these battles if you're a normal or immature believer. But now, you are cruising above the level of maturity. You are entering a different kind of realm. You are no longer in the natural realm, but you are walking in the supernatural.

Every rank comes with its pain. They say every promotion comes with a different kind of challenge, and that's what I'm saying. If I were to phrase it more accurately, I would say it like that. At this point, when you see many breakthroughs, it's not just breakthroughs that you see. I wish people could be more open about what they go through. Let's look at the book of Daniel and the three Hebrew boys. Even up to the point when they were thrown into the fiery furnace, they had already gone through some painful moments—painful moments where it feels like you're paralyzed. But then, you reach a point where you can't go back. You can only move forward, and at that point, you say, "*It's too much; it's too painful. Let death take me because I know my death is gain.*" Why? Because I know I will rest from all these things and go to my Father for rest. That's what I mean when you reach that point. That's when you know that your breakthrough is around the corner.

God sometimes allows people to go through a painful experience. That means you are in the fiery furnace, and you can never be normal again when you come out. For gold to be gold, it has to pass through the fire. So now you can become gold and are qualified to be gold. People like this will always serve God with fear and trembling, preaching repentance and warning others of the cost of ignoring the truth of God's word or choosing a word that only favors their interests. Those who have gone through the fiery furnace are careful with sin and their anointing. That's what it takes to be anointed by God.

I'll give my testimony and revelation. But first, let me say this: If we had seen the three Hebrew boys thrown into the fiery furnace and witnessed the fire physically, we might have cried for them. But to them, it was better because they wished for something different. To them, they felt it was better to die and rest than to give up their God and serve another god. For the children of God, death is gain, and life is Christ. But God met them when they were ready to give up.

I pray you may be strong enough to say no to what will compromise God's assignment for your life. The Holy Spirit also brought to mind the case of Jonah. When the fish swallowed Jonah, he must have thought, "*Now I can die and rest from all my troubles.*" There are times in life when it feels better to die because when you die, you know you're going to your father. Why should demons, witches, and wizards continue tormenting you on earth for nothing?

When the fish swallowed Jonah, and he was in the belly of the fish, I could see that he was thanking God. "*Let this journey end here. I know I'm going to my Father and will have permanent rest.*" The three Hebrew boys: You don't know what they went through until they were thrown into the fire. They were tortured physically and spiritually and drained emotionally. I mean this for those going through a serious deliverance journey—it's not easy. Before you even face the fire, there are painful moments. And I believe the Bible doesn't even tell us everything. As I walk on my journey of deliverance, and as the Spirit of God keeps taking me back to this, I see that it's the same thing I'm going through as I pursue my deliverance journey.

Look at the case of Daniel. You don't know what he was going through before he was thrown into the lion's den. Daniel made up his mind that it was only his God and no other god. He said, "*If you want to kill me, death is gain, and my life is Christ.*" He remained focused on his assignment, no matter what surrounded him or what he saw. Even though his adversaries wanted him to stop praying to his God and pray to their god, Daniel refused to do so. He went to the upper room, opened the windows facing Jerusalem, and prayed thrice daily.

Despite the commotion in Daniel's life, he found the strength to pray. He changed his environment to pray—he went to the upper room, a place above the normal level, where he called on the Spirit of God, asking for mercy. All the things he did were creative efforts to touch the heart of God. In other words, he was saying, *"I am tired. What can I do? I am trying to be creative in every way."* Even with his prayer, you could tell he was already in pain. He was emotionally drained, physically tormented, and spiritually tortured. Oh, Jesus. When we talk about torment, spiritual torment is real.

After all of this, it came to the point where they were putting him in the firefly furnace. His was the lion's den, and now he was like, *"Thank God, let the lion eat me so I can go to my Father."* Why? Do you think that was the will of the Father? Ask yourself: Why do I serve this God? You begin to think, *"I haven't done anything wrong. I've done all the right things. I've followed the principles of God. I walk righteously according to the Bible. There's no reason I should be going through this."* That's when the Spirit of God reveals that what you're going through isn't about you. It is related to faulty foundations. Why is it being shown to you? Because at this point, there is no battle you can't stand. That's when you rise and say, *"Let me do something. I know this could be too much, but now I know the truth, and I must do something."*

In the case of Daniel, he wished he could die and rest in peace. The Bible says it: Why should the nation say, *"Where is their God?"* Now, at this point in the deliverance journey, it hurts even more when nations mock you. You have to swallow everything because they don't understand what you see, what you're walking through. You are pursuing your God, and you know God is with you. Even the Bible says there will be a point when people will ask, "*How can you be a child of God and be tormented like that?*" How can you be a child of God and cry like that? How can you be a child of God and have the devil after you day and night, causing shame, pain, and disappointment?

There was a time I was tormented, not once, not twice, but many times. There's something we call a Faraday cage. God places a protective barrier around His people to shield them from the enemy's attacks. I know when I needed a Faraday cage, I was being tormented. They release torment when the enemy can't reach you through other means. It's like being squeezed, like every part of your body hurts— even your nails, your bones. You want to stay in bed because your body is in excruciating pain, but you don't know why. You didn't exercise or do anything to cause this. That's when you cry to God: "*Why do I have to go through this?*" But that's when Psalm 79 comes in. Even the nations ask, "*Where is their God?*" You begin to feel like a sheep without a shepherd.

At that point, you say, "*God, why do I have to go through this?*" And you wonder if you should even pray anymore. But that's when you say, "*Let Your will be done.*" Remember when Jesus prayed, "*Let Your will be done*"? That's the point I'm talking about. God, if this fire is to take me, hurry up; enough is enough.

When he was thrown into the lion's den, Daniel said, "*Let Your will be done.*" And that's when God intervened. He had no choice but to come through. People may mock you, but God may allow these things because He's already trusted you among the highly ranked heavenly soldiers. He will only allow you to face what you can handle, even though it's painful.

When we sit down and discuss all the spiritual battles we've gone through, some of these things may be hard to understand. It's better to see someone physically hurting than to experience the unspeakable torment of spiritual warfare.

Oh, Jesus Christ. Let me tell you, I respect deliverance. I will do whatever I can to help many. God is with us, and we are almost there. In those times when you feel like you've done everything right and the warfare intensifies, even when you don't know what's fighting you, remember: Deliverance is not a joke. It's deep-rooted, and it's not for everyone. Deliverance is for the chosen with a special septum to deliver foundation, territories, and Nations in the name of Jesus.

God is taking all the glory. As long as He knows He can get the glory through you, He will take you through anything you can handle, for He has tried you and tested you.

Conclusion

My Battle in life was the battle for the chosen. Through these battles, I have discovered that I am also a preacher, a deliverance minister, an eagle Intercessor, a warrior, a watchman, a God's mouthpiece, and an end-time revivalist. It started as a family matter, but through life's battles, it gave me a microphone on a global platform from the pulpit. What the enemy meant for evil, God has turned it around for my Good and the good of my family.

God's desire for you is not a life of struggle, defeat, or endless oppression. He has not called you to live in the shadows of bondage, nor has He destined you to be a prisoner of forces that seek to steal, kill, and destroy. His will for you is victory—a life marked by freedom, joy, and the power of His presence working in and through you. Christ has already secured this victory, breaking every chain, silencing every voice of condemnation, and triumphing over every force of darkness that once held you captive.

But victory is not automatic. Although Christ has made it available, the price has been fully paid, and though your prison doors have been thrown open, you must decide to step out. You must choose to walk in the freedom that has been purchased for you. It is not enough to know that deliverance is possible; you must take hold of it. It is not enough to hear the truth; you must act on it. Every revelation you have received, every principle you have learned, and every truth illuminated in your heart must now be applied with unwavering faith and obedience. Deliverance is not a passive experience; it is an intentional pursuit. The enemy will not simply step aside and allow you to walk into freedom unchallenged. But you have been given the authority to claim what is yours.

The chains that once held you have no power unless you allow them to remain. The voices that once tormented you have no authority unless you give them room to speak. Every oppression, every cycle of affliction, every stronghold that once ruled over you has already been defeated in Christ. Now you must rise in the strength of that truth and declare that you will no longer be bound.

It is time to step forward, to reject fear, doubt, and complacency, and to silence every lie that says you will never be free. It is time to take up the armor of God, stand firm in faith, and walk in the fullness of what Christ has made available. Your freedom is not in question—it has already been won. Your victory is not uncertain—it has already been secured. The only question that remains is whether you will lay claim to it or refuse to settle for anything less than the life God has ordained for you.

The door stands open! The chains are broken! The enemy has been defeated! Now, child of God, step into your victory. Live in the freedom that has been given to you. Walk in obedience, move in faith, and never again allow anything to take from you what Christ has made yours. Victory is not a distant hope; it is your present reality. Now, go and enjoy it.

- Acknowledging Robert Henderson books on the Courts of heaven was such a helping tool on completing my journey of deep foundational deliverance.

www.ingramcontent.com/pod-product-compliance
Lightning Source LLC
Chambersburg PA
CBHW051139120626
46547CB00012B/867